SPIRIT OF THE EMPTY HAND
by Stan Schmidt

Editors: Randall G. Hassell
Dale F. Poertner

FOCUS PUBLICATIONS
St. Louis, Missouri
USA

Published by Focus Publications
P.O. Box 15853
St. Louis, Missouri 63114 USA

© 1984 by Focus Publications
7th Printing, 1994

ISBN 0-911921-00-2

Printed in USA

"If you want to know balance, walk the tightrope."

Acknowledgments

The contents are a revised version of a Master's dissertation submitted and accepted by the University of South Africa. I express my appreciation to:

- my karate teacher, Masatoshi Nakayama *Shihan* and the instructors of the Japan Karate Association for revealing to me an exciting world of possibilities;
- my supervisor, Professor M. van Schoor, for his sparks of inspiration, and to the lecturers and staff of UNISA, Communications Department, for their kind help;
- my wife, Judy, family and friends for their love and support;
- my colleagues and students in the martial arts for providing a healthy environment of enthusiasm, rivalry, and growth;
- my typist, Dawn Kermuir and Yvonne Goldberg for their proofreading;
- Dr. Frank Foulkes for clarifying many Japanese terms.

Finally, I wish to thank my friend, Dr. David Berson, for living through it all with me.

Foreword

Karate is a set of attainments associated with intense mental discipline. It involves poise and skilled movements. These, in turn, reflect a frame of mind, a philosophy of life, a mode of communication. At its best, when its' dashing and daring movements are executed with bravura and elegance, precision and clinical dispassion, intelligent anticipation and resourceful dialogue, it represents one of the highest expressions of the skilled use of the human body.

How has it come about that human beings are capable of developing such polished and poised physical achievements? The answer is to be sought far back in the history of mankind.

The human family have been upright walking creatures for some four or five million years. It was a remarkable achievement: Instead of the body being supported on four limbs, it was carried upwards in defiance of gravity to a stance and gait in which it was supported on only two limbs. To accomplish this, our remote ancestors had to achieve a new orientation of the body towards the pole of gravity. In dragging the front of the torso away from the earth's gravitational field and swinging it upward, through 90 degrees, humankind attained a stance in which the weight line passed in a plane through the two firmly planted feet. The back and front were nearly evenly balanced on either side of this plane—unless the person took to wearing high-heeled shoes, thereby throwing the weight forward, as though trying to undo four million years of evolution!

To adjust to this two-footed position, the human skeleton, ligaments, and muscles underwent change so that the body became well-balanced. Thus, upright standing and walking man requires less muscular energy to maintain this position over long periods of time than, say, an ape. It is true that an ape can stand upright for short spells, but the amount of muscular energy expended is great. This costliness of energy expenditure is simply another way of saying that bipedalism in apes is inefficient and leads to early fatigue; in man it is much more economical.

As the human's body framework became modified, the body's balance improved, and less and less muscular action was involved in the maintaining of the upright stance. Today, human beings need only delicate muscular flickerings to maintain uprightness even for long periods. We are able to maintain this position under a most extraordinary array of conditions: In a high wind; on a moving walkway or an escalator that tries as hard as it can to remove our delicately balancing feet from under us; on a tightrope, ice skates, or skis; or as a ballet dancer up on *pointes*.

It is man's trifling muscular input into the functions of standing erect and of relaxed walking on the level, coupled with the large extent of untapped muscular potential, that have enabled him to develop his bodily techniques in well postured, poised, and skilled movements—like those of karate. In fact, it has been a long-standing association and friendship with Stan Schmidt and with some of those he has trained that have helped me to reach some of these insights into skill. It was through watching him in action that I came to appreciate the all-important and pervasive influence of the brain behind the human hand, foot, and eye.

For it is a truism that, whenever we encounter them, skilled movements rest upon a dual basis: the structure and the use of the executive instrument—whether head and neck, trunk, or limbs—and the nerve center that on one hand appreciates the incoming messages from eyes, ears, sensitive fingertips, and on the other gives commands to the periphery.

Hence, karate is an intensely intellectual pursuit. It demands concentration, memory, orchestration, anticipation, judgment. For Stan Schmidt it has gone further. It is a form of communication, of non-vocal body language. Messages, warnings, friendly overtures, conversation, peaceful or aggressive intent, are flashed to the sparring partner by eyes, stance, muscular tension—as surely as by spoken word.

Mr. Schmidt has sought to understand, and in this book to interpret and transmit some of the eloquent messages of the body in karate. His interest in this aspect of karate led him to write, in 1981, a Master of Arts dissertation on "Karate and Communication." He subtitled it, "A Study in Human Awareness." In this work he showed himself to be not only a *karateka** of singular skill and prowess and a great teacher, but a subtle, sensitive, and perceptive interpreter of the meanings that lie behind the surface manifestations. Out of that thesis this book has grown.

Its immediate interest and relevance to practicing *karateka* and karate teachers will be obvious and compelling. It will, however, be of interest to a wider readership—to teachers, lecturers, and other educators who are concerned with the development of the body's potential and its loquacious messages; to all those physical therapists, athletes, dancers, gymnasts, and physical culturists who appreciate the living and immortal beauty of a shapely limb, but who realize that a shapely limb is useless without the mental discipline to cultivate, train and exercise it; to persons concerned with communication in the wider sense, including speech therapists, administrators, and readers. All of these and many others, I believe, will benefit by absorbing the message of Stan Schmidt's essay on awareness, communication, and karate.

Signed,

Phillip E. Tobias
Professor of Anatomy
President, Institute for the Study of Man in Africa
University of the Witwatersrand, Johannesburg
March, 1984

---

* *karateka* - karate practitioner/s

Introduction

Unarmed combat is as old as mankind. However, the term karate was coined during this century. It describes a system of empty-hand fighting that took root in Japanese soil in the 1920s.

The leading pioneer of modern-day karate was an Okinawan school teacher by the name of Gichin Funakoshi. He first taught his skills at a number of Japanese universities. His art flourished and rapidly became accepted as one of the newest of the traditional martial arts.

The island of Okinawa, which is today a province of Japan, was in earlier times a refueling and trading port as well as a market-place for the exchange of cultural ideas. When Japanese feudal lords overran the island and prohibited the inhabitants from possessing weapons, the environment became an ideal melting pot in which techniques of empty-hand fighting were tested, tempered, and developed.

The whisper that went across the land was, "Make a weapon of your empty hand."

Through a process of secret training and natural selection, a system of workable fighting techniques developed. These techniques, then known as *Okinawa-te*, were thus implanted by Funakoshi into a new environment, rich with centuries of experience in the martial way.

Okinawa's intriguing method of combat was enthusiastically digested by the keen-eyed Japanese, who infused into it their well known heritage of vigor, quality, and strategy. Thus emerged the new karate—a fast-moving, streamlined, potent art—the human being as weapon, bare of any technological extensions.

In the 1950s, the USA and South Africa were among the first Western countries to receive official instruction in the art.

Since 1963, more than a quarter of a million people have studied karate at various *dojos** throughout the Republic of South Africa.

In the past decade, the popularity of karate has spread across Europe and the rest of the Western world. A vast network of *dojos* and international associations have been established, and these are the prime media for propagating the art. There are a number of independent styles of karate with individual technical differences, which may be compared to the various disciplines in ballet. Despite the differences, the common denominator throughout the styles is that they all adhere to a curriculum involving systematic training in the three prime elements of karate, viz., *kihon,** *kata,** and *kumite.**

Karate is not like a school course that terminates after a period of years. It is an ongoing process practiced by a total cross-section of society. Today it is the most popular of the Japanese martial arts in the Occident. The significance of this is that it has become a noteworthy medium for the communication and exchange of cultural assets. The role of karate in our society is still unclear to the public at large. To the trainees, it represents a number of functions. Some see it as a means of keeping fit while enjoying the sporting and competitive aspects. Others view it purely in terms of self-defense. There are a few who pursue karate as a do,* a way of life, which includes all of the above and much more.

Whichever way karate is used, it is a matter of individual opinion and needs. What is of importance is that it is being rapidly grafted into our society. We need to take a closer and more realistic look at it. Up to now the mass media have not presented the essence of the art.

---

* *dojo*—a place for learning the way
* *kihon*—basic techniques
* *kata*—formal movement
* *kumite*—sparring or fighting
* *do*—the way

Professor Phillip Tobias, head of the Department of Anatomy of the University of Witwatersrand, has made observations that relate karate to the development of the human being. He sees it as one of the crowning achievements of human skilled activity, in which neuromuscular coordination and mental discipline are most highly developed.

In this work karate is presented as a mode of existential communication—a play form that civilizes—with a potential for developing physical, mental, and emotional awareness in the participant.

Both the teacher and the student in part one are the experience of the writer, who was involved either directly or indirectly in what is described.

In part two, various play arenas of karate are examined. In certain of these arenas, discipline and control are the dominant themes, while in others, freedom and creativity prevail.

The karate participant experiences the ever-changing awareness of giver and receiver, recreating himself as each situation arises, under the guidance of the master who performs as both disciplinarian and midwife.

Author's Note

I intend to communicate some of the reality of the art of karate to you so that it lives in both of us. Instead of adopting a formal, objective approach in which dry, technical information is presented to you in a systematic fashion, I have decided to use a more interesting and real method.

The spirit of my message is that of challenge. I require that you participate and interact with me. I need you to be an active, responsive communicator who allows me to penetrate your inner world.

I am not asking you to necessarily accept my viewpoints, but I require that you actively consider and try to live them, temporarily, at least.

My challenge, therefore, is that you become a student (that is, for the early chapters) and that you remove your everyday clothing and dress yourself in *karate-gi** and *shiro-obi** and then imagine yourself stepping into the dojo as a student, your purpose being that you may gain the deepest understanding of karate-do.

According to Nakayama, "The greatest masters never cease to be students." This approach is pertinent to the Japanese way of life encompassed in the concept of *shu-ha-ri*. *Shu* represents the stage when one learns from tradition—this is an historical approach—but before one becomes too bound by tradition, one applies *ha*. *Ha* is to break the chains of tradition, and if the chains are broken, one moves into the state of *ri*, which is a state of transcendence, the freedom of the self to create and express itself. Shoji describe *shu-ha-ri* as a freedom from all restraints from the standardized movements.

Shu-ha-ri is an ongoing process of repetition and renewal. It has often been said that the Japanese have a highly formal and traditional culture. This would appear to be so, but there is a paradoxi-

---

* *karate-gi*—training suit
* *shiro-obi*—white belt (worn by beginners)

cal consideration of which most Westerners are not aware—that it is traditional for the Japanese to break tradition. The wheel remains a circle, but as it turns, it advances. This is *shu-ha-ri*.

It is in this spirit that I ask you to free yourself of past traditions, ideas, or biases in order to participate in a social institution, karate, which Nishiyama and Brown define as involving direct contact between two or more human beings.

This story is not entirely a work of fact, nor is it a work of fiction. It is not a personal autobiography, nor does it flow in a strictly chronological order. Despite all this, the incidents in this book are based upon my own experiences as well as those of my students and colleagues. The names of the masters are real. Other names have been changed but are based on real characters. The value of this story lies in the spirit it evokes within you. If it fails to move you, throw it away immediately!

Stan Schmidt

Chapter One

The First Step

It was with a feeling of trepidation that I ventured up the stairs of the Karate Centre. I had always felt the urge to take up karate, but somehow I seemed to lack the courage. Now, at last, something drove me up the stairs. I walked through the front entrance, enrolled at the reception, donned the overlarge-looking white *karategi*, tied the stiff-looking white belt around my waist, and feeling extremely odd and out place, entered the training area.

There were, in fact, two training areas. One, a spacious, shining wooden floor with a number of men, women, and children of varying ages wearing different colored belts. They quietly chatted and limbered up, waiting for their class to begin. On the other, smaller training area were the new white belts, congregated in a corner. I instinctively gravitated to them and apprehensively watched the more advanced *karateka*. The repetitive sound of thwack-thwack emanated from the far end of the large floor where a wiry purple belt was spiritedly striking a *makiwara*,** which vibrated and bent back with the force of each blow, returning dutifully only to be launched off again on its short, jarring journey. The regular, rhythmic cadence had a mesmerizing effect.

Suddenly, the sound of the buzzer cut across the *dojo*, transforming it into a hive of activity that ended almost as quickly. Everyone, including my group of white belts, was now seated in two lines facing the *dojo's* main wall, which was clear of all ornaments.

I was at the end of the back row, and those with darker colored belts were seated progressively closer to the right front of the class.

---

* *makiwara*—upright wooden board used for striking and punching

Two *senseis** wearing *kuro-obi** crossed the floor and then knelt facing the front wall. The senior student at the far right of the class commanded, *"Mokuso!"** A short period of silence followed, and then he announced, *"Yame."** The two *senseis* turned to face the class and the senior gave the command, *"Sensei-ni-rei,"** much like a sergeant-major directing his troops to battle. The class and the *senseis* bowed to one another.

The chief instructor's serious face broke into a smile as he welcomed the new students to the *dojo*. He paused, then added, "Train hard and regularly, and you will grow strong in many respects." As I attentively listened to the *sensei*, I felt twinges of pain in my ankles and thighs. It crossed my mind that this Japanese way of sitting was somewhat awkward. The *sensei* continued that we no doubt wondered what the meditation and the bowing were all about, and asked why we shook hands with people when we met.

"To greet them," answered an eager-faced boy, wearing a yellow belt.

"That's a good answer," nodded the *sensei*. "However, the Japanese way of greeting and entering into a relationship is by bowing. The handshake and bow are both rituals that introduce or conclude any form of personal interaction. Have you ever noticed the rituals of various top artists or sportsmen? Bjorn Borg looks at his opponent, then meditatively bounces the ball a number of times before he serves. This activity prepares him psychologically for the forthcoming confrontation. In the karate situation you bow to one another before and after an interaction. This bow conveys mutual respect and signifies that you offer and accept the challenge of both training partner and situation. The bow between teacher and students also signifies mutual respect. Further, through your bow you

---

* *sensei*—teacher or professor
* *kuro-obi*—black belt
* *mokuso*—a command to meditate
* *yame*—a command to stop
* *sensei-ni-rei*—bow to the teacher

are implicitly communicating that you will sincerely immerse yourself in the training."

With these words, the *sensei* stood up and handed the class over to a sub-instructor who gave a short command, "Class positions!" I found myself going through a series of arm-swinging, leg-stretching, stomach, back, arm, and leg exercises, generally known as the warm up. The instructor explained that white belts should do each exercise only as many times as they could manage. Every repetition was punctuated by a mystic sounding, yet motivating, set of utterances: "*Ichi, ni, san,*"* and so on, which I later learned was counting in Japanese.

Lying on my back, opening and closing my legs, I became aware of the mixed group with whom I found myself. Next to me was a young, dark girl smoothly and lithely doing her exercises, while on the other side of her was a thick-set man, probably in his forties, puffing and blowing with much effort. To the front was a small boy who was so taken in by the sub-instructor's movements that he kept throwing himself off balance in his enthusiasm to emulate him. As I changed to the press-up position, drops of sweat splashed on the floor. I became more fascinated by the design the droplets formed on the floor than by the realization that my fellow students were all so different.

I became extremely conscious of my own breathing, which was deeper and faster than normal, while in the periphery of my mind it occurred to me that the *dojo* represented a micro-world situation.

As the class changed into a sitting position, with one leg forward and the other curled up to the side, the wall clock told me that *only* 15 minutes had passed. The sub-instructor made it look easy as he quietly urged the class to gradually stretch and breathe. "Every part of the body must be strengthened and stretched," he said. "To work only one area of the body is dangerous. Okay, relax." He looked up and told us that some people train only their stomachs, forgetting about their backs, which comprise opposing muscles. He illustrated

---

* *Ichi, ni, san*—counting, one, two, three, in Japanese

how the stomach and back muscles may be compared to the guy ropes of a tent. If the front side becomes too strong, the result could be an injury to the back. "The aim of karate," he said, "is to convert malposture into poise through balanced exercise."

He concluded the warm-up by bowing and handing the class back to the *sensei*.

At this point I felt about ready for a shower. The *sensei* called the white belts over to the smaller floor area while the rest of the *karateka* began moving across the floor doing a series of blocks, kicks, punches, and strikes under the strict direction of another instructor.

The purple belt who had been striking the *makiwara* was the driving force of the class. A focused and intense look of concentration on his face was coupled with supple limbs that transported him dynamically across the floor, always a split second ahead of the other members of the class. While his body moved lithely as a unit, each blow emanating from his driving hips made a crisp, snapping sound akin to the crack of a whip. At the completion of each one hundred repetitions, the class rested for a few seconds, then proceeded with the next technique. My group was totally absorbed with this interesting variety of forward, backward, and sideward movements.

"That class is going through what we sometimes call the alphabet of karate," commented the chief instructor. My group was awakened from its reverie as he continued, "Like words, or letters of the alphabet, each technique fits into a total pattern that allows you to form the language of karate. The Japanese term for these basics is *kihon*. As beginners, the major part of your initial training is *kihon* training.

"Before we start with *kihon*, one must understand that there are certain psychological attitudes that are intimately related to defending oneself. These attitudes concern the mind and the spirit. For example, look at that class in action and observe the performance of the green belt over there. Now compare him to the purple belt. They both have excellent form, both are artful and well coordinated, but if you are aware, you will notice a significant difference."

The *sensei* turned to us, inviting comment. A tall, well-built, foreign-looking student instantly answered, "He has got what it takes," pointing towards the purple belt whose creased face was covered in perspiration.

"We call that fighting spirit," nodded the *sensei*. "Good form is not enough. The fighter needs something more. For example, take an empty gas bottle, which has a specific form. When filled with compressed gas, it has something more, a potentially explosive content. It is your spirit that comprises the content, like a fire within you. We must train ourselves to develop fighting spirit."

"We will begin with *kihon* training. Please make two straight lines facing me," the *sensei* commanded. After much shuffling and bumping into each other, we eventually achieved two uneven rows. A sulky individual to the immediate front of me had not been particularly cooperative. He persisted in standing out of line. I was not sure whether he was purposely doing so or not. The *sensei* politely requested, "Lucas, will you please move into line?" Each of our names was printed clearly on the left lapel of our karate suits. Lucas obeyed almost begrudgingly, and I felt somewhat uneasy and irritated by his indolent manner. The *sensei* fired a question at the class in general: "Why have you taken up karate?"

"To learn to defend ourselves," ventured Mannie, the thick-set man. Jack, the small boy, added, "Also to get strong." Similar answers came from other members of the class, including myself, confirming the main theme, self-defense.

The *sensei* walked to the front of the class and continued, "In every lesson you will be confronted with physical challenges as well as mental challenges." Suddenly his attitude became more compelling. He stood facing us with feet shoulder width apart, appearing ready yet relaxed. His eyes had a flash of strength in them. He invited various members of the class to come up to him and push or pull him off balance. The tall foreigner, Nick, pushed the *sensei*, who was unmoved. Others in the class tried and could not break his balance. Lucas had one try, and he was unable to move the *sensei*.

"Try harder," taunted the *sensei*, and Lucas responded by jumping and beginning to pull the *sensei's* arm, but suddenly he changed tactics and gave a powerful shove. In a flash, the *sensei* rotated his hips and shoulders like the side step of a bull fighter, and Lucas was left plunging forward and staggering off balance. The *sensei* remained in his relaxed standing position. "This position I am in is a natural standing position, a position of readiness. Whenever we use the term *yoi*, please assume a ready position."

He immediately commanded, "*Yoi!*" and we breathed in and out trying to coordinate our legs, arms, breathing, and bodies into a state of awareness. He repeated the exercise a number of times and stressed that in a state of *yoi*, one must not let one's mind wander. "*Yoi* is more than your body appearing as if it is ready. As you stand in a ready state, you are like a cat about to attack its prey...tensed, yet relaxed...a combination of hard steel and soft fur.

"Be ready for anything," challenged the *sensei*, as he stalked through the class. I became more tense as he approached me. He paused, then moved to the front of the class. "Good; it is in this state that we practice karate. Our sense of awareness needs to be far higher than that of the average individual." He extended his hands forward, palms upward, to form an apex in front of his chest. We all imitated him. He slowly and methodically rolled the tips of his fingers to form two compact fists with his thumb curled firmly across the index and middle fingers. We followed. He inverted his fists, placed them together with palms facing downward, and with both arms horizontal, he aimed towards the front center member of the class. The knuckles of his index and middle fingers were both more prominent than the other two. "Like spearheads of war," I thought. As we all achieved this position, the *sensei* smoothly drew his right fist backward, rotating the forearm so that the elbow formed a point that traveled directly backwards. He finally stopped as his upturned fist reached his waistline, against which it snugly rested.

As we imitated him and reached this same position, he continued by returning the same fist on a forward journey to meet its mate again. The action was well synchronized with the inside of the forearm lightly making friction against the side of the body. We struggled t master this forward-back technique as we continued to repeat it many times, following his example. As we began to co-ordinate and exhibit correct form, he gradually fed us with additional information.

"Relax your arm as you begin the blow and allow the out breath to coordinate with the extending action of the arm. Now tense the hips and stomach and finish the out breath as the fist reaches the end target point."

As I continued, the tiredness that had crept up on me vanished and I felt my punch becoming crisper because of the added correct breathing.

"*Yame*! That means stop," he explained.

We relaxed our arms at our sides, assuming the *yoi* position again.

"Please try to realize at this point that although *yame* means stop, you must still be in a ready state."

At this, we braced up and tried to look alert. It was obvious that most of us were overdoing it. I felt quite tin soldierish as I tried to imitate the *sensei's* poise. Apparently I was trying too hard, for he looked my way, remarking, "Do not over-tense."

We continued for a further fifteen minutes. "Our final exercise is similar to the first," he said, as he assumed a stance called *kiba-dachi*.* We were told to form a circle and with the sensei in the middle, we all aimed towards him and completed 100 *choku-zuki*.* This had us all puffing, but the *sensei* was not satisfied. "We will do it again, but this time give a loud *kiai* at the end of each 10 repetitions." We looked at him questioningly. "The *kiai*," explained the sensei, his voice dropping to almost a whisper, "is a shout from the pit of the abdomen." As he spoke, he called us close to him and continued in a modulated voice, "The *kiai* is an outward expression of one's inner fighting spirit." suddenly, there was an ear-shatter-

---

* *kiba-dachi*—horse riding stance
* *choku-zuki*—straight punch

ing noise, "IYA!" causing us to jump with fright. We felt stunned and confused. Quite calmly, the *sensei* returned to the same quiet tone as if nothing had happened. The *sensei*, amused by our reactions, chuckled with relief; we laughed. Immediately, he shouted, "*Yoi*, form into a circle." Now we were alert. We exhibited this by instantly reforming a circle. Again, we repeated the 100 punches, and as we *kiaied* uninhibitedly at the end of each 10, it was if this shout acted as a booster to our spirit, for as we executed the last 10 repetitions, the class was working in unison like a powerful threshing machine. We were all highly stimulated as the *sensei* said, "*Yame*." He told us to line up and sit quietly in meditation. "*Mokuso*," he directed. I felt the perspiration rolling down my forehead, nose, and cheeks to my chin and onto the floor as if emanating from a hot, tropical spring. Inside my steaming head was a buzzing collection of thoughts and images. A minute or two of silence passed, and the *sensei* ordered, "*Yame*! This meditation is your private time. A time of calmness, a necessary contrast to the high peak of action you reached during the training. It is useful from the physical standpoint because it allows your stimulated body to return to normal. Psychologically, too, meditation gives you time to reflect on what you have achieved, or wish to achieve. It is s a time of self-examination and self-control, a time to be at one with yourself. We conclude every class by repeating aloud the five maxims of karate. These maxims—character, sincerity, effort, etiquette, self-control—are psychological elements that direct and strengthen the karate trainer in his quest for self-defense. They are the ethics of true martial arts. Gichin Funakoshi conceived the maxims. He once said, 'The karate man never strikes the first blow and thus it should never be used unless in the cause of justice.' The maxims are the civilizing function behind this deadly art."

The *sensei's* serious, commanding tone penetrated my consciousness. I sensed the profundity of his words. As I left the *dojo* floor, undressed, and stood under the refreshing shower jet, the resounding echo of the maxims vibrated across my consciousness: character, sincerity, effort, etiquette, self-control—an echo of the past...a premonition of future aspirations...maybe.

Chapter Two

A Road of Air, Earth, Water, and Fire

Two months had passed, and the beginners class, which originally consisted of 20 members, was now 15 strong. Five had fallen by the wayside. Was it too demanding, or was it for some other reason?

Lucas, Lisa, Jack, Mannie, and Nick were still present. We were approaching the twentieth lesson. I now felt able to express the various *kihon* movements more fluidly with less tension and strain. Although my body was trimmed down and had become stronger and more agile, the training was still tiring, confirming the *sensei's* statement that as one begins to gain strength, so one will tend to put more energy into every move.

The arm movements I had begun to master more quickly than the kicking. The *sensei* called me aside one day after he saw me struggling to get my side kicks higher. "You need to concentrate more on stretching and limbering exercises, at least 30 minutes a day. As you become more supple, you will need less stretching time. It will become a pleasure as you become looser." He explained that the muscles and not so much the tendons and ligaments needed to be stretched gradually and systematically.

Watching Lisa easily placing her legs above her head made me envious until after talking to her she told me she envied my power. I began to realize that we all have weaknesses that must be recognized and worked upon. Although I was not satisfied with my suppleness, my groin-height kicks had at least improved to waist height.

At the end of our twentieth lesson, the *sensei* called us together for a discussion. During the past 19 lessons there had been little talk and much action. Although he started gradually at first, he had progressively added more repetitions and extra techniques. He explained, "You are now acquainted with the four major stances, five major blocking techniques, four important striking and punching techniques, and five basic kicks. In addition, you have learned methods of shifting forward, backwards, and sideways. You are learning how to strengthen and stretch parts of your body correctly, and you have an understanding of other important elements such as breathing, correct tension and relaxation, coordination, and the importance of training to achieve a higher state of awareness.

"I can already see a big change in all of you, but how do you feel?" We all agreed that we had changed. Nick echoed the attitude of the class in general, "*Sensei*, I do feel much better; it is all becoming clearer, but mainly I feel that I have got such a lot to learn. For instance, I am not happy with my balance. I am always losing balance as I move backwards."

The *sensei* nodded, "Yes, Nick, I am sure that all of you are experiencing some problem or other. Karate is not an instant thing like coffee. What causes pain now will become more of a game later. The Japanese samurai, who were among the nobility between the sixth and eighteenth centuries, had an interesting expression that illustrates this concept. In describing their activities, they did not say as we do, 'I did that' or 'I live life.' They would say, 'I played that' or 'I play at life.'

"Karate was brought to Japan by Gichin Funakoshi in the earlier part of this century. It was implanted in an already flourishing environment of the traditional skills and spirit of *budo*,* which comprised the martial arts of *kendo*,* *judo*,* *sumo*,* *kyudo*,* and many others. Gichin Funakoshi often said to his students, 'Before endeavoring to become victor over another, one should endeavor to become a victor over oneself.' When you can achieve this, you will

---

* *budo* —military way
* *kendo* —swordsmanship
* *judo* —grappling
* *sumo* —stylized wrestling
* *kyudo* —archery

experience few battles with others. This is what I have to say to you all as you leave the beginners class. From tomorrow, you are all promoted to the general class where you will begin to train and interact with people who are more experienced than you are. It is like moving from your back yard to a public park. In other words, you are going to have to cope with the demands placed on you both by the instructor and your fellow students. Enjoy it. *Osu!*"*

The apprehension that I felt upon entering the general class soon disappeared as we were relegated to the far end of the group.

"Your immediate challenge is to learn the *kata, Heian Shodan,*" explained the *sensei. Heian shodan* consists of 21 moves done in a set sequence. The *sensei* carefully taught us each move. Then we practiced the *kata* over and over again, softly. As we became more coordinated, so he encouraged us to put more focus into the moves. Mannie, from the very beginning, was very tense and put full effort into each move, only to be cautioned by the instructor that he should relax more and gently coax his limbs and body into the right groove. The *sensei* warned that if a faulty technique was done with force, it was quickly learned by the neuromuscular system. It would then become difficult to learn it. He encouraged us to work in an air-like fashion. "Become air and let your limbs and body be light so that they can move easily. Find the correct course."

As we achieved better form, so he allowed us to occasionally use more tension and become like earth, solid and powerful. He stressed that we develop form and then power, in that order.

Mannie could not distinguish between earth and air. He was tension personified. Because of this, he took longer than the rest of the class to learn the *kata*, and he was continually exhausted and flushed.

"I find it hard to relax," he told me in the change room. "I am not a ballet dancer," he chuckled, "and that's what they want us to become."

---

* *osu* — a colloquialism conveying a host of meanings to generate spirit

I agreed with him that I found it difficult to master the appropriate balance between tension and relaxation. I recalled the *sensei* telling us that the *karateka* was to master a number of important elements. Firstly, we needed to develop good form. This meant seeking the most efficient way of executing each technique. But, without flexibility, it was difficult to achieve form. The next important element was strength. However, the *sensei* cautioned that tensing unneeded muscles at the wrong time acted as a brake and weakened the force of a blow. Intimately related to strength is correct breathing and coordination, which are the next important elements. Thus, using the weight of one's body combined with form, strength, and speed, the karateka aimed at achieving the surprising and often elusive total power called kime. *Kime* for the martial artist is not mere physical power. It is a totality of body, mind, and spirit focused at the point of impact. *Kime* requires peak performance in one and all of these areas. Great sportsmen such as Gary Player produce *kime* when they rocket the ball into the heavens.

At long last we were allowed to do *kihon* and *Heian Shodan* together with the class. Training with the higher group was stimulating. Towards the end of the class, each belt level group had to perform their particular *kata* in unison while the rest of the class watched.

There was a particularly strong group of green belts who were able to execute *Heian Yondan* in synchronization. Watching them made us white belts enthusiastic, and we tended to over-rush the moves of *Heian Shodan*. After each performance, the instructor made a remark or two, which we came to know as the good news and bad news.

"You have shown strong spirit, but please try to go lower in your stances. Keep the center of gravity down." Staying low in my stances was greatly tiring, and I forever marveled at how easily young Jack rooted himself down like a racing car with a wide wheel base. We ended the class with each belt group doing their particular *kata* six times. At the end of the class, the *sensei* invited questions.

Lucas bluntly stated, rather than asked, "The *kihon* training is fine and I like the *kumite* that the colored belts do, but why do we have to do so much *kata* training?"

"You will be doing plenty of *kumite* in time, but only when you are ready," answered the *sensei*.

"*Kata* training, as you will later discover, is more valuable than you realize." He went into a fascinating description of what *kata* meant.

He explained that *kata* is a series of moves much like a theorem of self-defense. "*Kata* training," he continued, "is the mind part of karate, giving one brain time. It introduces the student to the powers of visualization and preparedness, much like the lawyer who prepares his case before entering court. *Kata* contains numerous possibilities of attack and defense. It is a fight against imaginary opponents." He cited Jack Nicklaus' approach to golf as an example of *kata*. Jack Nicklaus, before a tournament, invariably walks through the course studying the environment and likely problems. He is already playing his match before the tournament begins. The *sensei* explained that *kata* fires and trains the imagination. We were intrigued to learn that there were more than 25 *katas* in our style of karate, some with as many as 120 moves. "These *kata* contain the secrets of self-defense. It is for us to explore them," he said, "and discover the wisdom of self-defense."

The *sensei* told us that the Japanese feudal lords overran the island of Okinawa, south of Japan. They banned all the inhabitants from bearing weapons. The folk were often waylaid by robbers or attacked by wild animals. A silent call went across the land: "Make a weapon of your empty hand." In secret places and in the dead of night, people trained, exchanging ideas and techniques, some of which had been learned from sailors from passing ships. These travelers were from parts of Asia, China, and Formosa, where various forms of fist and foot combat developed.

Among the secret trainees of empty-hand fighting was a young student, Gichin Funakoshi, who later worked as a school teacher and finally became the pioneer in Japan of what is today known as karate. He coined this term early this century. Many Okinawans molded, trained, and hardened their limbs into formidable weapons. They applied their empty hand techniques to actual self-defense situations, and through a process of natural selection, successful methods of self-defense were woven into *kata*, each of which became a living record, or storehouse of fighting wisdom.

"By doing these *kata*, we are practicing traditional methods of combat that have proved successful in the past. Once you are accomplished in these traditional forms, we then encourage advanced students to develop their own ideas; thus, karate becomes an art. It is an ongoing process of repetition and renewal. We develop, not in a circular fashion, but rather in an upward spiral, always returning to the basics. But before I get too deeply immersed in the philosophy of karate, let me now tell you that you will all be required to undertake a grading examination in four weeks time."

I felt my heart suddenly banging against my chest.

The *sensei* continued, "The new white belts are all acquainted with *kihon* and *kata*, but there is a third part of karate that you would be examined on, *kumite*. Don't worry, the *kumite* at white belt level is highly formalized, a step by step learning of how to block and counter single blows delivered first to the head area and then to the stomach area. This method protects weaker persons, allowing them to gradually develop into strong and confident fighters. If, for instance, we had everybody immediately doing free fighting, the strong would defeat the weak, the result being physical and psychological damage. However, through systematic *kihon kumite*,* the degree of difficulty, skill, and pace is gradually increased so that the students are given time to develop and discover hidden strengths within themselves. Tomorrow we will begin with *kihon kumite*. Sleep well tonight."

The Monday class seemed electrified. The *sensei* took us quickly through a warm up, then 10 minutes of repetitive *kihon* and straight into *kata* training. By the end of 20 minutes, we were perspiring when he halted the class, and with a curt, short-clipped command,

---

* *kihon kumite*—basic sparring

he ordered, "*Naotte*."* We knew what was coming next, and we quietly waited for the inevitable. Suddenly, "*Yoi*, form into two lines facing each other."

This was it, my first confrontation and the person facing me was an imposing, wiry, tall green belt. He I had previously evaluated as being the silent leader of the dynamic green belt group. I felt weak-kneed as his eagle stare bored into me. My eyes, searching for some relief, wandered down his chin to his lapel, where seven bold, black, threatening letters S-T-E-P-H-E-N held my gaze. A stray thought sneaked into my mind just as the *sensei* ordered us to assume the starting position, "What am I doing here?"

"*Gedan barai kamae*,"* commanded the *sensei*. Stephen snapped into *kamae* even before the *sensei* had finished. I was supposed to stand rock still, ready to block the forthcoming attack to my face, but his sudden get-ready action caused me to lose balance and shuffle backwards, increasing the distance between us. Like a magnet, he instinctively moved closer again.

The *sensei* ordered the class to announce *jodan*, which means that the attacker is warning the defender that he intends to step forward and do a straight punch to his head level.

"*Jodan*," shouted the attacking side in unison. Again this caused me to overreact and shuffle away from my attacker. Again, he closed the gap instantly.

The *sensei* directed, "Attackers do five *oi-zuki*,* defenders step backwards doing *age-uke*.* After the fifth block, do a counter-punch to just short of the attacker's ribs. Do the first set softly, like air." He smoothly counted, "*Ichi, ni, san, shi, go*."

I was pleasantly surprised that I could see and block each of Stephen's blows. On the return journey, I tried to move like air. He smoothly blocked my attacks. We practiced in this way many times

---

* *naotte* —a command to relax
* *gedan barai kamae*—a command to assume the basic ready position
* *oi-zuki*—stepping punch
* *age-uke*—rising block

guided by the instructor's count, which had a caressing tone to it. I started to enjoy myself and began to develop a sense of confidence.

Then, "*Yame*. Now we will do *chudan** attacks and the defenders will step backwards blocking with *ude-uke*.* This time put substance into your blows. Be like the earth, rooted down and powerful, and keeping your good form, fill yourself with tension. Don't try so much to hit your opponent. Become immovable and solid. This is a form of isometric training, holding your power."

Stephen suddenly transformed from a body of lightness into coiled spring steel. His warning shout, "*Chudan*," totally echoed the wound up state of his physique and immediately created tension within me. Not deliberately trying to hit me, he stepped forward methodically and locked into the *oi-zuki* position. As my blocking forearm met his extending arm, I became aware of his inherent strength, because my arm bounced ineffectually off his, causing me to stumble and lose balance. I repositioned myself for the next blow and tried to put more power into the block, but again I tottered, losing balance. The more we practiced, the more frustrated I became. I sensed that "the machine" in front of me contained some human element judging by the faint glint of pleasure in his eyes.

The sub-instructor stopped us and explained to me that I was using only arm power. "If you can generate power from your legs and hips, maintaining a connection between all of the muscles and joints of your body, then your block will begin to express the power of *ki*.* Your separate parts should join together and rotate as a whole."

I managed to do a little better with this guidance. I couldn't get Stephen's arm to waver, but at least I wasn't losing balance any more. Lucas, to the right of me, appeared to be faring better than I. From the periphery of my vision, I noticed that he was challenging

---

* *chudan*—middle level (abdomen)
* *ude-uke*—forearm block
* *ki*—intrinsic energy flow

a yellow belt rather excessively. The yellow belt looked totally exhausted. Lucas, I imagined, had let a couple of blows go through,
and the yellow belt was struggling to keep a safe distance between
them.

The *sensei* called us together, explaining that we should now
adopt a third approach. "Try to become water. Move your hips and
block with a smooth motion, letting your blow flow out of the
movement. Don't hold back. The attacker, in a relaxed way, must
allow his blow to follow through to his partner's abdomen. On the
other hand, the defender must be alert and move away from the
punch, blocking it. Protect yourselves," he added, looking towards
our line of defenders. He continued, "In this type of *kihon kumite*
the attacker may try to make contact. This is because he has
warned you what he is about to do, and the fact that he is allowed
to make contact, causes the defender to become alert. It makes the
interaction more realistic and tension-provoking, which is what
self-defense is all about. Of course, if your partner is a small child
or girl, don't go out to crush their ribs. Use discretion."

Facing each other once again, Stephen's countenance changed.
He had a relaxed look about him that caused me to relax, and that
proved to be a mistake. Before I knew what was happening, his
mass closed in on me, and I felt a dull thud on my stomach...and
another...and another. It was obvious that he was not trying to hit
me hard, for I could feel he was holding much of his power in re-
serve. Thinking that I must redeem my loss of face, I went at him
hammer and tongs, very unlike the character of water that the
sensei had asked for. Surprisingly, my first blow struck him in the
stomach, but he nonchalantly brushed off the next four.

By the time we had started the fourth concept, fire, I was breathing heavily, and my cheeks were burning from the effort of this
repetitive confrontation. In retrospect, I realized that Stephen was
actually playing a game with me.

"Fire," described the *sensei*, "can be seen in many ways, but for
now try to become the lightning bolt, a special kind of fire. Try to
be in a quiet state, then suddenly explode towards your partner,
immediately becoming calm again."

This time Stephen's face looked like the Mona Lisa's. A little voice inside of me said, "Don't be fooled; this man is dangerous." But the very fact that I was communicating inwardly made me blind to blow that was over before it had even started. The skin on my stomach was stinging. Then that Mona Lisa face again, then another blow to the same spot.

"I must do something," I said to myself, "Don't let the Mona Lisa smile distract you. Become lightning!" On the third and fourth attacks I did not block, but I managed to accelerate my body backwards so quickly that the blows were short. I felt elated, ready for the last blow, but now Stephen waited. I was eager to get it over with, but he just waited. Would it never come? I had a few false get away starts, over-anticipating his attack. He calmly waited, poised in the ready position, not in a hurry. I felt the blow before I saw it, and this one caused me to catch my breath and bend over forward. The *sensei* de-winded me with a sharp slap on my back. "Learn to block," he commented, smilingly. Looking at Stephen, he chided, "Was that fair" We are supposed to be training on the fourth concept, fire, but didn't you use the concept of 'void' on that last blow?"

"*Osu, sensei*, I am sorry," apologized Stephen, bowing deeply.

Feeling somewhat shaken, I was relieved when the *sensei* called all together. I needed this respite.

"Void is the fifth approach to fighting. We will not deal with it today. It is too advanced a concept at this stage. Let us once more go over the first four concepts with other partners."

Lisa was my partner this time, and we were able to practice the concepts in a less tense situation. We both found it difficult to express all four ideas adequately. While I felt I was typical of the concept of earth with my naturally solid physique, Lisa was flexible and able to flow like water.

As I left the floor that evening, Mannie and I spoke enthusiastically. "What a fascinating experience that lesson was," I said.

"Very demanding," he observed. "There is so much to learn."

"Well, I just found out that I am not a total man."

"Why?" he asked, laughing.

"Because I am only a quarter of a man—an earth man."

With four weeks to go before the grading examination, the pace was stepped up. After the warm-up we went into 15 minutes of *kihon*, a short rest, then an equal period of non-stop *kihon kumite*. After another short rest, the white belts repeated the 21 moves of the first *kata* at least 10 times before we were told to warm down to end the lesson.

The higher-graded members remained on, because they had extra kata to do. John, the purple belt senior of the class, had explained to me that with each step up the grading ladder, the *karateka* is given one extra *kata* to do. The yellow belts who are on the first rung must be proficient at *katas* one and two, and so on, up through orange, green, blue, and purple belt. The purple belts (fourth kyu*) must know katas one to five, plus a further power-building *kata* called *Tekki Shodan*.

The present training period was nearly at an end when the *sensei* called me and told me that I had qualified to enter the forthcoming gradings. I learned that a number of members of my class would not be grading, as they had not satisfied the requirements of having attended at least 30 classes over a minimum period of three months.

---

* *kyu*—student level

Chapter Three

The First Grading Test

It was Saturday before I realized it. I had arrived at the *dojo* one hour before starting time. I wasn't alone, for the place was already filled with examinees. The odd butterfly or two I had felt when I awoke now increased to a swarm as I noticed the empty row of tables and chairs that faced the *dojo* floor. Another change to the traditional face of the *dojo* were the intriguing markings that had been taped onto the floor in red and white. These strategically placed lines and crosses were to me ominous symbols of the unknown. The *sensei's* final words to us the day before, "Don't worry, you will soon find out what it is all about," had an unnerving effect on me. That night was spent wrestling with images. "What if I slipped and fell, or worse still, if I could not remember my *kata*? I had better do it right now. On with the light. Okay, I know it. Back to bed. But what direction will I be facing tomorrow? I am used to doing the *kata* facing the front wall of the *dojo*. What if we have to face another way? I must sleep now. I need energy tomorrow. In *kumite* I will have to work against somebody. What if it is Stephen? I will not let that man make a fool of me in front of all those people. Let him try his fancy tricks on me. I'll show him. It's not fair. He's a green belt. I'm only a white belt. Just let him touch me, and I will go berserk."

In frustration, I exploded, striking out and kicking in all directions at my imaginary adversary. I stopped when I realized that I had sent the bedside lamp on a journey to the far corner of the room.

On the way to the *dojo*, I kept singing the first line of that song, "Oh, what a night it was...it really was, such a night."

On the hour, the *sensei* walked onto the *dojo* floor followed by three other men smartly dressed in the association's blazer and tie.

John *sempai** gave us a quick command to line up. We faced the examiners, bowed, and were told that our white belt group would be first to be examined. We were called in two's. Lucas was my partner.

"To start with, we will examine you on *kihon*. Do each of the basic techniques three times stepping forwards. Start with the *oi-zuki* or lunge punch. On your third move do a *kiai*. Then turn around and do the next technique, *age-uke*, rising block, and so on through the syllabus ending with *yoko-geri kekomi*, side thrust kick, moving sideways."

The *sensei* had taken us through this drill numerous times, yet my palms were perspiring and my heart was beating wildly as Lucas and I, the first two on, stepped into the ready position.

Suddenly, it was over. Now we were facing the examiners, our chests heaving from the over-effort.

"Do *Heian Shodan*, first *kata*."

We returned to stand on the starting mark, Lucas on the white cross and I on the read cross.

"Try to finish on the spot on which you start," indicated one of the examiners. This was a distraction I did not need. It was hard enough to remember the sequence of the *kata*, let alone doing it powerfully, but now I was also expected to finish on the cross. There was no time for a practice run, for an examiner had already said, "*Hajime*."* As I finished the last move and returned to *yoi* position, I could not resist looking down. Had I really done the *kata*? Surprisingly, there was the red cross directly under my feet.

Before I could gather my thoughts, the examiner pointed to two parallel lines, which were about 18 inches apart. "Face each other standing on the lines," he ordered.

This was *kumite*, or five-step attack and defense with a partner. I toed the line, bowed to Lucas, and tensely took up the ready position. From the corner of my eye, I noticed that the examiners

---

* *sempai* — senior
* *hajime* — a command to begin

were busily writing on what must have been our examination cards. Perceiving Lucas' determined posture, I remembered that the *sensei* had stressed how important it was to exhibit fighting spirit when one worked against an opponent.

Every technique between Lucas and me seemed to end in a deadlock with neither of us getting our blows through. We blocked so spiritedly that in our over-tense state, we never reached the prescribed target, which was the face and stomach, in that order.

"That will be all," said the *sensei*.

We bowed and moved off the area uncertainly as the next two examinees approached the starting line. I felt frustrated and so did Lucas as we whispered to each other in the far corner of the *dojo*. Between whispers, we watched Nick and Mannie go through their paces.

":They are doing well," remarked Lucas.

"Better than I did," I added.

When all the white belts had finished, we were lined up in front of another table. The *sensei* had our examination cards in front of him. To our left, the yellow belt group had just begun with their gradings.

"You have all been promoted to eighth *kyu*, yellow belt. Congratulations. You have made satisfactory progress. Collect your certificates at the desk and please study the remarks on your examination cards. Each of you have certain strengths and certain weaknesses."

My remarks revealed some interesting and surprising results. For most of my *kihon* moves I received five, which is the symbol for required standard. However, for my side kicks, I had four, which meant my kicking techniques were poor and needed to be improved upon. I was pleased I had not one three, which means a fail. For my *kata* I was slightly better than Lucas. He had five, and I was five point three. Our *kumite* marks surprised us the most. We both had six, which signified excellent for the level of eighth *kyu*. Although we both felt we were over-tense, the examiner had written, "Good spirit" opposite our marks for *kumite*.

Later, at a nearby cafe, some of us gathered and discussed the grading. Jack came to each of us proudly showing us his six for *kata*, while Lisa had a six for her side kicks. She had a four for *kumite*. Nick and Mannie achieved an average five, except for Mannie's side kicks, for which he received a three point five.

Mannie and I decided that we should in the future meet 20 minutes before class to do extra suppling exercises.

Chapter Four

Training
Gasshuku—Renewal of Spirit

The months passed by and the general class had become like a second home. It was no 18 months since that first white belt class. There were some more of those tense confrontations with Stephen and with John, not to mention Lucas, my partner from the original white belt class. But, things change. It was different now. Some months ago John and Stephen had been promoted into the black belt class and no longer attended the general class. In a way I missed them. Lucas and I were now fourth *kyu*, and we shared the leadership, giving the commands to bow, and motivating the general spirit. Leaders today, but what of tomorrow? At the cafe I talked to Lucas and the others about the forthcoming *gasshuku.**
Karate, I had found, was like going on an unending adventure. As one progressed through the belt levels, there were always new and intriguing challenges. This *gasshuku* idea was again something new to us. I had, however, on the odd occasion overheard certain senior *karateka* speaking in hallowed tones of the hardships and unusual experiences they had enjoyed on *gasshukus*. This idea of enjoyment can only be appreciated in terms of karate experience and spirit. For what we as *karateka* enjoy is often looked upon as insanity by the average individual.

At work a colleague asked me what the word karate meant. After giving an exposition of the many complexities of *kata*, *kihon*, and *kumite*, I ended by telling him that the word karate meant empty hand. He almost fell over with glee as he chortled, "Empty hand?

---

* *gasshuku*—special training (usually out-of-doors)

Sounds more like you guys have empty heads." I vowed never again to try and explain karate to a layman.

I marveled at Jack, animatedly talking to Lisa. He had grown taller and the signs of a lithe, muscular frame were beginning to show themselves through his white, tight-fitting tee-shirt. He was on the verge of manhood, but already comported himself like a man. Lisa, Mannie, Lucas, and Nick looked well, but especially Mannie. He had, I felt, undergone the most change. Compared to the burly yellow belt days, he was now lean and sinewy. That extra 20 minutes a day had done wonders for both of us. We weren't anywhere near Lisa's level, but Mannie and I could split down to within 20 centimeters of the floor, an improvement of about 10 centimeters. The instructor was right; muscles can be stretched. We had systematically worked on our hamstrings and abductors and had included various exercises to supple our backs.

Nick reached across the table and tapped me on the shoulder. "Are you still with us?"

"*Osu*, I am with you," I reacted. "What do we need for the *gasshuku*?"

Nick had a list that the *sensei* had given him. Two days previously, the *sensei* had left for the mountains. He would spend one week alone on his *gasshuku*, "emptying his cup," as he put it. John had told me that the sensei did this at least once a year. He took with him no luxuries, no watch, no radio, nor computer, only the bare necessities—sleeping bag, food, water, some reading and writing materials, a guitar, and a portable *makiwara*, which he strapped to a tree trunk. His existence involved doing what he felt attracted to doing and that, I am told, included not doing.

John had at one time spent a day alone with the *sensei* in the mountains. While striking the *makiwara*, he said, "Do what you will," and then in a relaxed manner, continued striking the *makiwara* for what seemed to be the entire morning. As John began cooking lunch, the *sensei* disappeared, returning a few hours later carrying a huge log across his shoulders.

"Tonight the fire will be our friend," remarked the *sensei* as he laid down the log and took an ax to it, neatly cutting it into smaller pieces.

"You are late for lunch," John said.

"Out here I have no lunch time, John. I eat when I am hungry and sleep when I am tired."

Saying this, he smiled, turned around and walked off to a nearby stream where he stretched himself out on a clean, white, flat rock like some huge, lazy cat.

We were all to join the *sensei* after his fifth day. The following two days were to be filled with hard training and hard resting, we were informed.

"The purpose of *gasshuku* is to make a breakthrough in spirit," the *sensei* had told us before he left. You will succeed in doing things you never dreamed you could achieve. For example, on one *gasshuku* we did 70 *kata* nonstop on river sand. It is a matter of breaking through various pain barriers and realizing the inner strength that lies within all of us. Don't worry (those words again), your purple belt group is ready for it. I am looking forward to seeing all of you in one week." With that, he bowed and was gone from the *dojo*, but the knowledge that we were going to have to perform next Friday and Saturday at the *gasshuku* kept us going. We had decided that we would accept everything with which the *sensei* might confront us, and not let him down. After all, we had heard he would be training along side us, and what better inspiration could there be than that?

Our purple belt group traveled together in a minibus and we rendezvoused with *karateka* from other *dojos*. We had traveled 120 kilometers and were surrounded by rugged countryside.

John, now a *shodan** black belt, was waiting as we arrived. At last we found ourselves in a tree-surrounded clearing, to be greeted by the smiling countenance of a very brown and very healthy-looking *sensei*.

---

* *shodan*—first level black belt

"*Osu*, welcome!" he shouted, guiding our vehicle into a camping spot that seemed tailor-made for our needs.

The ridge of the huge mountain to the west of us was beginning to darken in shadow as we finished setting up camp and lit our fire. I felt at peace, sitting on a flat stone watching stray flames lick upwards around the boiling kettle, while the sizzling sounds of steak added to the symphony of crackling fire, crickets, and modulated voices from the various camps.

The undulating sound of a nearby waterfall became the steady pulse upon which lively night sounds waxed and waned. It all sounded good, smelled good, and I felt good sitting together with my friends. We had been told the *gasshuku* would commence the next morning at sunrise.

As I sipped coffee, my gaze penetrated the very depth of the fire, and time stood still. For the first time in my karate experience, I felt no anxiety for the morrow, only a joy at being totally immersed in the present.

The first rays of dawn were hardly visible when a loud, clanging noise awakened me. I sprang up from my hard resting place on the ground and peeped out of the tent. John, already dressed in white *karategi* and black belt, was striking a circular steel plowshare going, which was suspended from a large wild fig tree. Within seconds the camp was alive with *karateka* briskly abluting themselves and changing into *karategi*.

We lined up sitting and facing the waterfall as the yellow gold of the sun appeared, growing steadily out of the rock-crowned mountain.

"We are off now on a two-hour breakfast run," explained the *sensei*. A line of 30 half-awake "karate suits" followed the *sensei* as he jogged along the river's edge towards the nearby mountain slope. The pace was comfortable, but as we progressed, the terrain became unpredictable. We moved along from loose sand to slippery river edges onto hard rocky surfaces. I became wide awake after bumping my head on a low-hanging branch of a tree. Just as I was thinking to myself, "Two hours of this?" the *sensei* called, "*Yame*."

We were on a wide expanse of water-worn rock and following the *sensei's* example, did repetitions of press-ups, sit-ups, and limbering and stretching exercises. Fifteen minutes later we began winding our way up the mountain again. Every 10 or 15 minutes we stopped and did more stretching and strength exercises. By the end of one hour we arrived at a huge, jutting shelf of rock overlooking the valley in which our tents nestled. The recesses of this rocky shelf contained a most prolific and luscious variety of green and brown fern life. My legs and lungs were burning from the climb. "A perfect spot for meditation," the *sensei* observed as he directed us to sit and quietly take in the scene.

My strength and energy rapidly returned as I sat peacefully amidst this harmonious setting. The reality of nature with its paradoxical character of contrasts captivated me. The sharp, jutting rocks were softened by the green ferns and oozing water.

Where strength and endurance took us up the mountain side, our return journey demanded balance and skill. Like a herd of mountain goats, we leapt and sprang our way down from rock to rock, stopping every 15 minutes of exercise as we did on the way up. The *sensei*, we learned was causing us to interact with nature, to communicate with our environment. As we neared our camping home, we ran the final 10 minutes carrying a rock in each hand. My shoulders, forearms, and hands felt lame as we reached the camp. I grew to know my "pet rocks" intimately and was relieved to empty my hands of them.

"The breakfast run is over," panted the *sensei*. "Use the stones for a pillow or for your fireplaces or whatever you please. Enjoy breakfast. There are three more training sessions today. The next one begins mid-morning. The gong will tell you when. In the meantime, discover the best way to relax and rebuild your energy. *Osu!*"

It was interesting sharing this experience with my *dojo* fellows. While eating breakfast, I realized how tightly knit our group had grown. We worked well together. In a short time we enjoyed a five-star breakfast in the most pleasing of surrounding. I had laid out and turned our little camp into a home away from home: a kitchen, sculler-bathroom, washing line, dust bin, and dining room *cum* lounge combination. The bedrooms were two tents—one for the men and other for Lisa and two other girls. All we lacked was a private toilet. If you needed to answer the call of nature, you took a spade and walked. Lisa and the girls washed the utensils and set the table while Lucas and Jack scouted for wood and kept the fire going. Nick chose to be the chef. We unanimously awarded him a six rating. Mannie pointed out that Nick, although an excellent cook, happened to be a messy one. He thus took it upon himself to keep our camp in a clean and livable condition aided occasionally by myself.

After breakfast, most of us lay and rested in the shade of four trees that protected our site. As I dozed, I realized that we had not yet made social contact with the other groups. To the side of the main camp clearing, a number of *karateka* were taking turns kicking a football towards a goal formed by two trees. The goalie was giving a dazzling display of acrobatic saves. One he missed, and a fellow commented, "Neville, you're slipping up." I dozed off and thought of the long day ahead and the *sensei's* advice about resting. Neville's way of resting was somewhat unusual, I felt.

Halfway through the second training session, I was so tired that I wondered how I would ever manage to get through the two afternoon sessions. We formed into a circle; half of us were in the shade of a clump of trees, while the other half were exposed to the sun. We had been doing repetition work and had reached our 2,000th count. The only rest came at the end of each 500 blows when the sun-drenched group changed places with those in the shade. This took 30 seconds, and the wearying count continued.

My *gi* was sopping wet. The only time the *sensei* spoke was when one of us counted badly. Badly meant softly, dispiritedly, uncleanly, or with disjointed rhythm. Moving clockwise around the circle, each counted in turn to 10, at which point the group *kiaied* loudly in unison, and thus we continued. Each person counting yelled out the accumulated score at the end of 10 counts, "*shichi, hachi, ku*, (seven, eight nine), 2,420!" uttered a weak voice.

The *sensei* reprimanded the culprit. "That count lacked spirit! While counting you are the leader; it is your task to inspire and motivate us."

"*Osu!*" we shouted, and continued with renewed spirit and vigor. The *sensei* looked tired, yet he did every repetition with us.

Lunch at our camp was a totally liquid one, consisting of any clear drink on which we could lay our hands. With a bloated gut, I flung myself to the ground and lay there, dead to the world.

I gradually came to realize that the irritating ring in my head was John's virtuosity on the steel plowshare. Dazedly, I arose and plodded towards the group who were gathering around the *sensei*. "More torture," I thought, "but it does not matter any more. I am numb from head to foot, so I just won't feel it." Looking at each of us in turn, the *sensei* spoke, "Each of your groups has kept much to itself up to now. In the next session you will begin to communicate with one another."

"Ah," I thought, "how nice. This session must be a talk session. Considerate of the *sensei*."

"This communication," continued the *sensei*, "is getting to know each other through the language of *kumite*."

I should have known. I resolved always in the future to expect the worst. My recent experience had taught me that should the *sensei* decide to give us anything less than the worst, this lesser of the two evils would be like a bonus.

The *sensei* explained that we would run for a short distance and then practice the various one- and five-step formal sparring interactions. Then we would run to another spot in a different terrain and repeat the sparring. "Always with a different partner," he stressed. Rising to his feet, he added, "Very different to *dojo* training, eh?"

"*Osu!*" we responded.

It was as if I was existing in some timeless zone. Like in a dream, a constant running over hills, under high forests, through water, stopping again, the interaction of limbs, changing faces, a cloud of dust, splashing water, uneven terrain, and automatically moving on again. I felt no pain. It was as if my body had disappeared and I was sparring with an unending line of spirit beings, their dust-filled paws and shining eyes so clear.

I lay gazing up through the widespread branches of my camp tree, spying an eagle high up in flight. Could he see me, I wondered?

"This session will last less than one hour and it will end today's training." The *sensei's* voice seemed far off as I stood together with the others in even rows on a flat, green surface facing the western hills. For the first half of the session, he taught us the moves of *Hangetsu kata*.

"*Hangetsu* means half moon," he explained.

"It is a contrasting *kata* with both sharp and gentle moves in it. It is a way of endeavoring to experience the hard and soft or *yin* and *yang* of which the Chinese speak. If you look, you will see that the setting sun and the rising moon are now both visible as we stand here."

True. I had noticed that *sensei* always related his teaching to the reality of the present time.

We trained *Hangetsu*, assisting one another in getting accustomed to its nature and moves. At last the *sensei* told us we would finish with *Hangetsu* done once only. But first we must meditate and visualize the truth of *Hangetsu*. "Try to express it from a state of openness or void, and let it happen," he said. "Let it unfold and allow yourself to harmoniously blend the elements of earth, water, air, and fire. If you can achieve this even to a small degree, you have communed with nature, and the essence of your art is thus beginning to emerge. Your one *Hangetsu* is like a painting that disappears as it is completed. You cannot hold or cling to it. Every sunset is such an example of our Creator's art. Now forget all techniques and teachings and become at one with nature and express your true self."

I did not consciously feel myself start the first move of the *kata*. It was as if I, instead, were being expressed. I was the setting sun. I was solid earth underfoot. I became the eagle on high and then the vibrant waterfall. I moved as easily as the fresh wind that now cooled my face. For the first time, I faintly experienced some understanding of the aphorism, "I was at once both artist and work."

Although the core of our training was still *kihon*, *kata*, *kumite*, and calisthenics, the second day was different from the first. The early morning session opened with the *Heian katas*, one, two, three, four, five, then *Tekki Shodan* and *Hangetsu*, 10 times each— a total of 70 *katas*. We had a short rest of about one minute after each 10 *katas*.

The two hours, although tiring, were not exhausting. I had a new-found energy, and *sensei's* approach was stimulating. For the first time, the *sensei* asked us to do the *kata* lightly but with good form as if we were air. The second time he demanded that we breathe strongly, vibrate our bodies and limbs, and root ourselves, capturing the character of sprung steel, which is an extension of the earth concept. Earth training is the expression of inner strength, but the stress of this approach had to be washed away by the third approach—water, which the *sensei* describes as a continuing wave or flow of power in which one freely released one's energy outwards, instead of directing it inwards. With earth one halted each blow and held and developed one's power in isometric fashion, whereas one became like water when one flowed smoothly from move to move, letting the weight and the speed of the body take one along a path. "Hitting as if one were water is one of the most devastating of outward powers," stated the *sensei*.

He told us of the time he had trained with the Japanese expert, Nishiyama *Sensei*, in America. Nishiyama explained that when hitting a large target like the body, a long, penetrating blow was highly effective. On the other hand, when attacking an object which itself vibrated at a high frequency, the blow needed to have a sudden shock effect, a snapping type of action. The human head was such an object.

"Thus," explained our *sensei*, "one generally follows through like water when attacking an opponent['s body. In striking the head, however, a fire approach is effective. Lightning is the fastest form of natural fire. It is short and sharp, and it does not have to deeply penetrate its target."

Before going on to the fourth approach, the *sensei* gave us a graphic demonstration that clearly expressed the nature of each of these elements. The difference was amazing. He did *Heian Shodan* four times, each time demonstrating a totally different personality, but its essential character was still *Heian Shodan*. The first time it appeared as if he were being blown into the different positions. He looked light and fresh, moved easily and quickly, here and there, without much apparent effort.

But when expressing earth, it was as if he were rooted to the ground and drawing his energy from the earth. He exhibited a sense of grandeur much like the character of the globe to which he was so firmly attached. He seemed to breath through his feet. In the third exposition his stepping techniques seemed to be pouring energy outwards, as if reaching around the universe with each move an extension of the other—a water flow action.

When he became fire, we watched spellbound. A move. Stillness. Then a sudden explosion of two or three moves. Quietude. His face placid, eyes flashing. He was like a magician who kept surprising one with an ongoing set of tricks. A let down, then a shock, and so on.

He finished the kata and walked serenely toward us.

"One should be careful when practicing fire or earth not to overstate oneself. A man who continually takes on the character of fire will burn himself out. That is why there is the fifth concept, void. Void is freely missing the four ingredients and baking your own cake, so to speak. When you use them all as the situation demands, you will then begin to understand the meaning of self-defense."

These two hours gave me a deeper understanding of kata than I had achieved in all the 18 months of training, but I was having trouble every fifth time when we were each required to mix the ingredients in our own way. If my *kata* was a cake, I doubted if many people would have eaten it.

We ended the early sessions with the discussion next to the bubbling stream. I came to learn that the other *karateka* had both interesting ideas as well as problems. Common to all was a striving toward self improvement. Before breaking for breakfast, the *sensei* confronted us with a prickly question. Like his lightning blows, it caused us to react and straighten up.

"Do you think you are a boring person?" he fired. His tone and attitude spoke to each and every one of us. I felt he was talking to me directly.

"No answer, thank you," as an all-knowing, inscrutable smile crossed his lips. The Mona Lisa could not have done it better. I felt let down, yet as curious as Alice confronting the perverse Cheshire Cat.

He watched us for a moment and continued, "Carl Rogers, the famous American psychologist, once asked the question, 'with what sort of person would you rather be friendly—someone who is predictable yet unreliable or someone who is unpredictable yet reliable?'" A pause while we tried to digest the cryptic question. "Do you think that a warrior who is predictable would last very long?" Again a pause and very evident visual and audible signs that many individuals were aching to answer the *sensei's* subtly rhetorical question. The *sensei* raised his hand and then spoke, "Finding the right question is often more important than finding answers. Over the months we have been dealing with self-defense from a totally martial standpoint. Now let us look at it from a human standpoint. After All, of what use is the art of karate or for that matter any art, if it cannot enhance our daily lives?"

I smiled inwardly—questions, questions, and more questions— but what of the answers? He raised his arm and opened his hand. "What is this?" he asked. There was a silence. A smile crept across his lips. "You may answer this one."

"No doubt," I reflected, "this *sensei* of ours is surely a wily one." Someone answered, "An empty hand."

"Okay," rejoined the *sensei*, and with that he wiggled his fingers, stretched them out and rolled them into a tightly balled fist that he pointed towards us threateningly, "and what is this?"

"A fist," somebody answered.

"Is it useful?"

"Yes," came the reply.

"All right," went on the *sensei*, "what would you call my fist if it always remained a fist and never became an open hand?"

The answer from Lisa was spontaneous. "Deformed!" The group exploded in laughter.

The *sensei* nodded his head and as the laughter faded, he put this to us. "Is laughter not a response to a hidden truth, to a truth that stares us in the face yet to which we are often blinded? We all suffer from physical deformities to some degree or other. But what of psychological deformities? Remember, I asked you whether or not you are a boring person? Now I will be an example of a boring person if I go on for much longer. But, can you think of someone you know who is a fiery, boisterous, backslapping type of person? If you were promoted at the office or at school, this fiery type of approach in congratulating you may be acceptable. Instead, imagine you are sick in bed, feeling fragile, and in strides Mr. Backslapper who heartily tells you that you are fine as a deformity. Is not Mr. Backslapper's personality also deformed?"

"Mr. Backslapper needs softness as well as hardness," answered Jack, putting the message in a nutshell.

"Exactly, and don't we all!" said the *sensei*, rising and closing the lesson.

I had just finished munching on the last and most tasty bit of *boerewors** and downed a carton of fresh fruit juice when John came to our camp and asked if we would help him to set up the equipment for circuit training.

"This is rugged equipment," I remarked to John as we finished tying a stout rope that spanned two trees. A few yards off we constructed a similar apparatus. "What are these for, tightrope walking?" I wanted to know.

"No, it's for upward and downward agility development. Circuit training is mainly for developing the five powers."

I helped him strap a large padded canvas square to a young tree and asked, "Oh, you mean water, fire...?"

---

* *boerewors* —a type of homemade South African sausage

"No," he interrupted, "those are five psychological approaches to training. We are now going to practice the five ways of generating physical power. Any good sports coach knows what they are."

"What are they?" I asked, as we assisted the others in attaching half a dozen thick rubber tubes to various tree trunks.

"Oh, er...I am sorry. I thought you were acquainted with them," he apologized. "They are rotation, vibration, movement, upward action, and downward action. We do them all the time in karate, but the circuit training drills are specialized approaches to improving these five powers." I was intrigued.

When all was ready, the *sensei* carefully explained the procedure for going through the circuit. We would work in groups of three or six but not with members from our own group, if possible. We had to go through eight drills and spend 15 minutes of sustained effort on each drill.

For rotation and vibration we practiced back-kicking and *makiwara* striking. Leaping over a stick swung at one's legs and blocking a kick on landing was the next drill. We worked in threes and kept changing roles every 10 repetitions. This was for upward power.

In the next exercise one had to duck under a rope and then kick over it at someone who blocked the kick. Two people worked against each other with the third person counting. This was to develop downward agility.

Then came the thick rubber tubes, which were attached to the ankle or waist, and one proceeded to move either forwards, backwards, or sideways doing various techniques. This was designed to enhance moving power.

As for vibration, my body seemed to be vibrating of its own accord as my wobbly legs conveyed me back to the camp after the session.

The final session was totally stimulating and enjoyable. I had, during the rest period, fallen into a deep sleep, but I felt enthusiastic and energetic as we commenced target training under the shade of some willows. We each had two targets—a tree on one side and an opponent on the other. A canvas *makiwara* was attached to the tree. The object of he drill was to make contact with the tree target with as much force as possible, then change direction and deliver a focused blow to within one centimeter of one's partner's face or abdomen. This alternating target drill demanded extremely superior judgment, timing, and awareness. It placed one's partner in a highly dangerous situation, for he was required to stand poised, watching the oncoming blow without blinking an eye or flinching. The exercise became more and more difficult as the distance was gradually increased between the human and the tree targets.

"Both participants learn from this drill," explained the *sensei*. "The one learns to place a blow while the other is developing a faithful eye. One's sense of perception will grow, and that attacker's move will begin to look relatively slower. However, faith and strong spirit are needed."

At first the members of our group were over-cautious against the human target, but as we began launching ourselves more spiritedly into the attack, so our judgment seemed to improve. I found that when I worked with a partner who exhibited strong spirit, I responded to him and was able to put full effort into my blows. I found that I developed an empathy with most of the *karateka* against whom I worked hard. We motivated each other through our encouragement and feedback—"Come on, Martin, harder. That's better...keep your back straight...*osu!*" and so on.

A huge, clear rock pool fed by a tall slender waterfall was our final *dojo* area. We faced each other waist deep in fresh, cold water doing what the *sensei* insisted was essential to every fighter's training—reflex work. He preferred the term "responding."

"Everybody has reflexes," he pointed out. "An eyeblink is a reflex, but a wicket keeper who blinks as the ball ricochets toward his head will end up a sick wicket keeper."

We stood face to face. One partner was allowed to punch with the leading hand to the jaw or with the rear hand to the opponent's stomach. Each blow had to be separate, and no feinting was allowed. We were allowed to make light contact on the jaw and heavy contact on the stomach if the partner was not fast enough to block the technique. Although the atmosphere was extremely tense, it was periodically broken by nervous laughter from certain trainees who found the tension too overwhelming. However, the give and take was exchanged in good spirit despite the odd bleeding lip or winded tummy. These were seen as minor mishaps when related to the spirit of the *gasshuku*, now almost behind our backs. I recalled what John had said the night before. "Cuts and bruises heal, but a slip of the tongue cuts deeper than the sword."

The *gasshuku* ended on a high note—jiyu kumite*—on the rocky surface of the river gorge.

"Listen carefully," cautioned the *sensei* before we began. "I know that most of you have done very little *jiyu kumite. Jiyu kumite* is very definite communication between two individuals. In this respect, I see two distinct types of confrontation, namely friendly confrontation and unfriendly confrontation. This first type I like termed free sparring. This relationship has the character of two people engaged in relaxed, sincere, open conversation with each other, each interested in what the other has to say. A feeling of cooperation is prevalent, with no one trying to outdo the other. This is free sparring or conversational *kumite*. The second *kumite* I see as free fighting. The confrontation is antagonistic, an opposition of wills. In this type of relationship, the aim is to defeat the opponent through superior technique and strategy. You are now only permitted to do conversational free sparring. Anyone who breaks this rule will spoil the fine spirit of this *gasshuku* by causing injury. The terrain is dangerous; thus move appropriately if you are on sharp or slippery rocks. Your fighting should rather take on the quality of air and water. Allow your partners free expression, and do not worry about looking ridiculous. Control your blows, and be aware of your environment and your partner."

I worked with three different partners ending with the *sensei* himself. I found that most of the time I had to concentrate on placing my feet where they would not cause me to lose balance. Mostly, I felt like a clown going through a circus performance, but

---

* *jiyu kumite*—free sparring

gradually I learned that the objects in my environment could be used to my advantage. Once, when Lucas' long kick came towards me, I side-stepped, using a tree as cover. Facing the *sensei* was a crowning experience in more ways than one. He did not once strike at me. All he did was to advance in varying rhythms, using my time of imbalance or hesitation to capture my territory and cause me to retreat. We ended up in the water. I had backed into the pool. As the fine spray from the waterfall fell on me, I blinked. The *sensei* faced me, unblinking, there were droplets shining on his face. I had come to know him anew.

Chapter 5

The Early Morning Trainers—
A Glimpse of Things to Come

I knew I was a changed person when I again walked on to the smooth wooden floor of our *dojo*. Previous anxieties and fears, many of which were subconscious, I now realized had left me. My body moved easily, and I felt light of spirit.

A big target lay ahead for our purple belt group. It was our third *kyu* brown belt grading, which would soon be held at the central *dojo* for our area. We would, for the first time, test against purple belts from other *dojos* in our area, some of whom we had met at the *gasshuku*.

The *gasshuku* had worked to good advantage. We had entered a new phase. The main step-up in the level of our training was that we were for the first time about to engage in *jyu-ippon kumite*, which demanded not only a physical quality but an equally important mental effort.

It was explained that semi-free sparring was one of the most difficult steps to master. Up to now, our *kumite* had been formalized except for the one occasion when we sparred on the rocks.

In basic sparring, the starting distance between two *karateka* is fixed, and so is the attack. The block and the counterattack are prescribed by the *sensei*. He is teacher and guide to our every move. We start and end in formal positions, keeping deep stances and continuing to hold our counterattacks close to the target area until the *sensei* orders *yame*. Although this state of training is controlled, I came to realize that it had an important function in the systematic development of every *karateka*. We were learning to groove our techniques as the expert golfer does. By locking and holding various basic positions, our connection points, that is, between limbs and body, were growing stronger and more flexible. Our body structures were changing, becoming more muscular. Furthermore, the form of sparring gives one's brain time to absorb the important techniques, and by holding positions, we can both check ourselves and be checked by the *sensei* for accuracy, skill, and strength. It was most difficult for me to keep my foot close to the head level of my opponent without dropping the leg. Lisa's hips and legs were strong and supple, almost like arms. My foot would attack the face area and, while trying to hold it there, it would gradually waver, dropping to near my opponent's stomach. I found it tiring to hold it still.

"Nice. Keep it up," John once said to me. "Not only are your building strength, but courage, too."

The *sensei* called the purple belts aside after a class and offered us tea in his office. It was seldom that this happened. Something was afoot.

"Can you meet me tomorrow morning at 6:00 here in the *dojo*? You will be gone by 7:00."

We could all make it.

"Must we bring our *gis*?" somebody asked.

"If you wish," he replied, leaving us in midair as we went out to speak to one of the sub-instructors. We wondered what was in store for us but came to no firm conclusion. Said Mannie, "Hitchcock was a master of suspense, but this *sensei* really takes the cake!"

The morning was dark as I parked my car outside the unopened DOJO. It was 5:45 a.m., and my colleagues were huddled together on the steps of the *dojo*.

"Where is the *sensei*?" "I dunno, probably forgotten about us."

But then it happened. One minute to 6:00, and cars started to arrive as if in convoy.

"*Osu*!" we bowed to the *sensei* as he opened the *dojo* doors. He was followed by at least 15 robust individuals, one or two of whom I recognized as national champions and examiners at the various gradings I had attended. We bowed as each one passed us, and they returned the bow in a firm yet friendly manner. We waited. The *sensei*, having changed into his *gi*, called us and indicated that we sit on a bench facing the main floor.

"Must we change?" I asked.

"No, I want you to observe the training carefully. We are doing mainly semi-free sparring drills this morning. This is important to your forthcoming brown belt and future black belt grading requirements."

Then he and the instructors group went into a warming up drill. They instinctively followed him, and very little was said except a unified *osu* now and then when various members of the squad called for more skill in any one exercise. I noticed that all participated, all counted, all were free to motivate or offer constructive criticism, but the communication was brief and appropriate. The right to communicate was never abused.

Where the warm-up was conducted in an atmosphere of calm, the squad members literally exploded into action as the command for *jyu-ippon kumite* was given.

This was not conversational *kumite*; it was most certainly semi-free fighting with the accent on fighting. Within the first seconds of interaction, one man lay on the floor, winded by a stepping punch from Richard, a young seasoned fourth *dan* champion. Richard stretched him out, gave him a few firm pats and slaps, and they were soon back in the thick of things. I noticed that Richard's partner kept his arms closer to his body and his legs more bent in what was a classic fighting stance, like a spring ready to uncoil. He was not caught a second time, his reflexes seeming to have sped ;up instantly.

For a moment I looked at Jack sitting next to me; his eyes were like big saucers. I guess mine were, too. As the session progressed, I began to realize what an immense difference there was between formal *kumite* and semi-free *kumite*. I became at once demoralized and motivated by the actions of these purposeful "
gladiators." I noticed three major elements in *jyu-ippon* that were not present in *kihon-ippon*.

Firstly, the protagonists were not restricted to remaining on two fixed lines. After the attacker announced what area he was about to attack, the defender could move around and keep increasing or decreasing the distance. Thus, a new important element, distancing, was introduced. This increased the degree of difficulty, since instead of a static target as in *kihon-ippon*, the attacker had to home in on a moving target. This in itself made it very hard to succeed with one's attack.

I noticed the *sensei* himself against one of the seniors. He never blocked one attack--he merely changed his stance from a forward bent knee position to a backward bent knee position, and the blow narrowly missed him, but within that moment his counterattack was delivered, and ;he was once more calm and ready for the next attack.

The second difference between basic sparring and semi-free was the thorough way in which the instructors launched themselves into their attacks, ending in what looked like full contact to me, especially when they aimed at the body area. In basic sparring we were also allowed to make contact, but it was not the same. It was within the confines of exactly one step. These instructors were literally flying across the floor, their entire body weight behind each blow.

I did notice, however, that the tall fourth *kyu*, Wayne, a national champion, lightly struck his opponent on the jaw if he got through. He succeeded in breaking through his opponent's defenses many times. It was obvious that discretion was being used, for if these men had landed their blows fully, they certainly would have seriously hurt their opponents. Wayne's body moved like an avalanche, and many of his partners were thrown off balance by the concentrated movement even before a blow was landed. His control at the final point was quite apparent.

Although the attacker in semi-free is permitted to strike his partner after warning him of the intended attack, the defender on the other hand, is required to pull his counter blow short of contact; otherwise the result would be chaotic.

The third main difference I noted between basic and semi-free sparring was that the attacker also endeavored to deflect or avoid the defender's counter blow. Each was allowed one blow and each was endeavoring to outwit the other.

Suddenly, an attacker was swept to the floor by our *sensei*. A moment later, Richard did the same thing.

"Phew," whispered Jack, turning to Mannie for reassurance. "Are they allowed to do that?"

"They are allowed to do anything they like," answered Mannie out of the corner of his mouth.

We discovered later that in semi-free you are permitted to break your opponent's balance if you can before executing the one prescribed blow. As the class progressed, there were other differences. In basic sparring , we extended our technique and held it close to our target for a second or two. These seniors crisply snapped each technique back as it reached the target, much like the lash of a whip. Furthermore, they did not stand waiting to be hit. Their extended arms or legs quickly recoiled into a sprung position, just out of distance, reach for the next attack or defense. Their *kiais*, I noticed, were highly explosive and were uttered naturally, emanating from their outbreath action. I now realized I had been forcing my *kiai*, and thus I remained too tense for too long a time.

"Who were those karate men in front with you when you bowed?" we asked the *sensei* that evening.

"Some of the most senior *karateka* in the country, area heads and the like."

"We didn't realize you all trained so hard," remarked Lisa.

"The true *karateka* never stops training," was his answer.

And Jack, "What grades were they?"

"Fifth *dan*[*] and above," he replied. "All had been doing karate for more than 15 years."

"Do the instructors come every morning to that class?" asked Nick.

"There are about 20 of us who train every morning," explained the *sensei*, "but a lot of the others live far off and they come through periodically to work with us. Most of these instructors run

---

[*] *dan*—master level; grade or degree

their own classes in the outlying areas. Well," asked the *sensei*, "did you learn anything about semi-free?"

"*Osu!*" we affirmed and thanked him for the privilege of watching. From then on we practiced semi-free at each session. When the time came for the area gradings, I still felt inadequate. Mannie had his big toe bound in red masking tape; Lisa had a crepe bandage around her left wrist, and my thumb was stripped with clastoplast. All small but annoyingly significant injuries. When kicking, Mannie had forgotten to pick up his knee, as the *sensei* had told us so many times, and had stubbed his tow on the knee of his partner. Lisa had blocked a front kick from Lucas with an open hand, instead of with her forearm, thus spraining her wrist. I had punched at my opponent's abdomen without curling my thumb against the other fingers, and it had collided with my partner's oncoming fist and had come off second best. Some of us learned from our mistakes, but not I, for the very next day I repeated the same fault and there I was now waiting for the grading with a throbbing right thumb.

Chapter 6

Sleepless Nights and the Brown Belt Test

The area grading is a big move up the ladder of *karate-do*. [*]
Previously, we had been examined on a local scale. Now we were
to be tested on a provincial scale.

The night before the grading I performed what appeared to be
interminable mental gymnastics.

Grading is a measurement of value, but now it was not so much
the unknown purple belts against whom I would be tested, but
rather the sizable group of onlookers that disturbed me, and more
so because I recognized a good number of them as being students
from the general class of which I was a senior.

I kept running into the changing room to go over the *kihon* combinations, *Tekki Shodan kata*, and ;the semi-free attacks and defenses with Lucas, Mannie, and Nick. What worried me was that I
would be forced to use my left fist for most of the countering
movements since my right fist was far too painful to be used.
Neville, the goalie on the *gasshuku*, greeted us all like old friends.
He, too, had his problems. It made us feel better for he confessed
that he had overdone it on the *gasshuku* and bruised his hip, not
from the training but from ;the flying goal saves.

The examiners, some from the instructors' morning class, seated
themselves and within minutes the grading was in full swing. This
time I was not the first one on.

At last I was called, and to my surprise Neville was my partner.
We went through the *kihon* at a rapid pace. The rivalry was clearly
apparent as we forged ahead trying to be that split second ahead of
each other. Then we were told to move across to the *kata* lines and
almost immediately given the command to begin. For a moment,

---

[*] *karate-do* — the way of karate

during the mid-point of the *kata*, it occurred to me that this virtual stranger and I were working in unison. It was if we were Siamese twins, connected by an inner pulse from which I could not separate myself. As we ended the *kata*, a number of people started clapping, but the chief examiner politely reminded the onlookers that an examination was in progress.

The spell of our united relationship was broken as we were told to take up our fighting positions. We now confronted each other directly. I no longer saw Neville. I saw an opponent, a very determined looking one, and my entire being focused upon him.

The test was *jyu-ippon kumite*. Each was required to do six separate attacks--two arm attacks and four leg attacks. The attacker had to indicate the area (head or abdomen) he would aim for and which technique he intended using.

My opponent would be the attacker to start with, and my test was to ward off his single attack and score on him with a single, well placed counter technique. He had an unorthodox way of moving. Shouting *jodan*, he immediately stepped backwards and like a praying mantis swayed his upper body backwards and forwards. He gradually moved towards me, closing the distance between us. I held my position firmly, not retreating a centimeter. Suddenly, he lunged forward, and I felt a tap on my chin. My block was a fraction late. I countered with a kick that fell short by at least 10 centimeters of his agile, retreating frame. "He is one up," I thought.

As we walked back to our starting points, I reflected on how Stephen had, in a similar way, tricked me as a white belt. Preparing to attack again, the mantis resorted to similar tactics. This time I stood firm until he had nearly reached the critical distance, and matching his subtle advancing motion, my feet moved, holding an appropriate distance. He lunged forwards, aiming at my abdomen, but my downward block and counter punch was well-timed. A murmur came from the onlookers.

The *mae geri** slipped through my block. I countered to his abdomen just as his kick struck mine. We were both a little shaken up from the exchange, and we became wary of each other.

My opponent, I felt, definitely had the edge on me. I was set on turning the tables as I advanced on him calling, "*Jodan!*" about to do my first attack. Momentarily, my mind envisioned the instructor's morning training and Wayne's avalanche attack. History was about to repeat itself. I pressed my hips forward, aimed them at the swaying entity in front of me, and took off. The mantis retreated. My right foot sensed the situation, and it switched from its forward motion to a short, sideward sweeping action, causing him to fall. As he fell to the floor, my momentum allowed me to drop forwards and finish what I had started. I was back at my ready position before he could think of countering. The onlookers responded but immediately hushed one another.

As Neville got up and face me, I wondered how I had managed to get that right and if I would ever be able to do it again. One thing was sure, much as I tried, I was not able to repeat the "miracle." He was a skillful tactician with an undaunted spirit, and our next five confrontations ended in a deadlock.

As we bowed to each other and to the examiners, the onlookers ventured a short burst of applause.

A number of *karateka*, including Neville congregated at the refreshment bar afterwards. Neville and I were talking animatedly when John placed his hands on our shoulders and spoke. "Congratulations! You both showed fine spirit." Then he looked at me and said, "Did you know that sensei want you to join the black belt training squad s from Monday? This means that in about nine months you will be eligible to go for firs *dan* black belt."

"What about the others?" I queried.

"They need a little more time in the general class, but they will be joining you within the next month or two." He paused, then added, "Lucas, I think, will be with you very shortly. He has a

---

* *mae geri*—front kick

problem of overreaching, which I am sure he will conquer soon. Isn't that so, Lucas?" he smiled, sitting down next to him.

As usual, the atmosphere was alive.

"How are the two fighting cocks?" called Mannie to Neville and me. "Before you fall too deeply in love, can I ask you something?"

We laughed. "Of course!" we both replied spontaneously.

"Is this another one of your unison tricks?" he teased, and becoming serious, he asked, "What became of your sore thumb?" and turning to Neville, "and your aching hip?"

"I forgot completely about it!" replied Neville.

"And," went on Mannie, now trying to look very serious and turning to me, "what became of all that left-handed training you and I did in the change room? It was as if you had three right hands on that floor today."

We laughed, and I wondered why the pain, which was returning to my right thumb, had been nonexistent until now.

Chapter 7

A Visit From the Japanese Juggernauts

The black belt club classes to which I had been invited to train numbered between 20 and 60 members. The majority of black belts, I was told, were first and second *dans*, with a sprinkling of third *dans*, and one or two other higher graded members. The 20 to 30 brown belts that trained in the class were there only by virtue of invitation. This senior class training was held every day of the week, mostly in the evenings.

Although we trained in the black belt class, the brown belts (third, second, and first *kyus*) worked mainly with one another, unless invited by black belts to train with them.

The Monday night class was full. Everything happened quickly and efficiently. As we started the *kihon* training, I immediately felt the difference in pace. I was behind the others all the time. Although the first part of the *kihon* was very basic as in the general class, the second part left me almost stumbling over my feet trying to master the different sets of combinations. A short demonstration by the *sensei* was followed by the class executing the combination five times slowly, then at high speed. The combinations started from a fighting stance to which I was not yet accustomed.

Where the *kihon* of the general class was like running, the combinations in this class were like fast sprinting. Although the *sensei* counted and motivated us during the sets, he allowed the other seniors to express their leadership during the resting period. Mike, a swarthy, dark fourth *dan*, was telling us to drop our center of gravity and keep it low as we moved forwards and backwards.

We paired off for kumite, but before I could bow to my partner, Stephen called me across to work against him. I was the target while Stephen performed 10 repetitions of each technique. Then it was my turn. He kept telling me to move more quickly and place my blows closer to his head or abdomen. "*Osu!*" I replied, but I wasn't going to tug too hard on the lion's tail.

"You are still holding back. Let yourself go. Only control at the final instant," he urged.

"Osu!" I tried again, but he was still not satisfied. "You must come harder at me."

The sensei had a very systematic approach. Next we had to repeat the same exercise, but this time on a moving target. As we started our attack, our partners had to step backwards, increasing the distance. Stephen's punches and kicks were so close that I felt a gust of wind on my face each time. He didn't touch me once except when he delivered a technique to my abdomen, snapping his blows against my karate suit or at most, against my skin.

When it was my turn, my blows were all far too short. I found it difficult to reach him as he moved easily backwards.

"You need to do more bag and makiwara training, changing your distance all the time," he told me as I finished the last back kick.

We then had to do the same attacks, except that our partners blocked and countered. And so we trained at semi-free sparring for about 30 minutes. Stephen did a variety of counter moves. He restricted me, however, to doing reverse punch, back-fist strike, or front kick.

"First understand your timing with these three techniques before you try too many others," he suggested. For kata training we were placed in groups, and Mike methodically taught us the moves of the black belt *kata, Bassai Dai. Bassai Dai,* I discovered some weeks later, had been chosen by the *sensei* as my *kata.*

"*Bassai Dai* must become your best friend," advised Mike. "Do it every day, like brushing your teeth, a good habit."

I was amused but impressed by these senior black belts. Their speech was disjunctive, to the point, like their blows. Quite appropriate for the circumstances.

We were called to line up facing the third *dan* black belts. The sensei told us he would be leaving for Japan shortly to train at the *hombu** *dojo* in Tokyo. He and a small number of other seniors did this periodically, always endeavoring to improve themselves and thus raising the standard of the country.

"I am hoping that I will be bringing a Japanese team back with me to compete against our national team," he announced.

The buzz of excitement was stopped short by the command, "*Mokuso.*" After the meditation we were told we could go while the black belts gathered in a circle for discussion. I wondered what they were talking about.

With the *sensei* away, it was as if the roof of the dojo were missing. However, the seniors encouraged us to train harder than normal. "Let him really see the improvement in each of us. A lot can be achieved in five or six weeks." We agreed unanimously, and the fire was back in the class again. When it occasionally flickered and waned, there was always someone who revived the spirit. Each of the seniors had his own special approach. Mike did it by sheer example. If the spirit of the class weakened, he increased his pace, effort, and intensity of his *kiais*. Don, on the other hand, would stop the training, call the group close to him and quietly encourage us. "You have all got it; it is waiting to come out. Imagine you are Tanaka, the world champion," he coaxed. We had all seen Tanaka on film, and this approach had us moving like dynamos. John and Stephen had a direct approach. If the spirit dropped too much for their liking, they merely lined up the class and fought each in turn. They had that uncanny ability of tying up their opponents within seconds. The tension quickly returned by this method.

At the airport, we were impatiently awaiting the arrival of the Tokyo-Hong Kong flight. The sensei, with short-cropped hair and looking meaner than normal, emerged from the customs area. At his side was a man whose cat-like eyes took us all in with one glance. Not only did he look like something akin to a sleek panther, he also moved like one. This was Tanaka *sensei*, former world champion. Behind him followed a team of four dynamic-

---

* *hombu*—headquarters (head school)

looking karate athletes dressed in black blazers and gray pants. On their front pockets was a simple yet striking motif, a red circle set on a white background. A rising sun, Japan's national colors.

The tournament, where our national team would meet and fight Japan's national team for the first time in history, was scheduled for the coming Saturday. Previously, our *sensei* and other instructors from our country had trained and fought in Japan, but never had a Japanese team visited us.

The *dojo* was alive with excitement. Through the grapevine we heard that each team was training hard.

The *sensei* took our class a number of times. He was different. His actions were very sharp and clear, and he spoke less than usual. Stephen and John, who also trained in the early morning class, had told us that the *sensei* was full of unexpected tactics. But above all, we were impressed by his new speed. I was told that this happened each time he visited Japan. I kept wishing for Saturday to come.

The hall was jam-packed, every keen *karateka* being present to witness this event of events. How would our team shape up? We had been isolated for a long time from the rest of the world by two factors—distance and politics—and now this breakthrough.

The preliminary matches and demonstrations were interesting. Before interval, Tanaka mounted the rostrum with his demonstration team. He had the hall shrieking for more as he ended the demonstration, dispatching four opponents almost at once. Four lightning techniques were delivered within the span of one second. He bowed calmly, as if nothing had happened, and left the rostrum. His spirit lingered on. I turned to Jack sitting next to me and just shook my head in wonderment. He was bouncing around on his seat, unable to contain. himself.

The main event saw an equal sharing of wins and losses between the visiting *karateka* and our men. However, what impressed me was the way in which these Eastern men, who were often a head shorter than their Western opponents, were able to move in, out, and around, giving a colorful exposition of what the art is all about. They possessed a superb ability to sense the right time to explode into action. Both they and our strong-spirited team had the audience on their feet cheering.

The tournament had done something for me, something spiritual. Master Gichin Funakoshi's words now made more sense to me: "The ultimate aim of the art of karate lies not in victory or defeat, but in the perfection of the character of its participants."

As we filed out of the auditorium, I realized that I would visit Japan in the future. But first, I needed to prepare myself.

Chapter 8

Breaking Boards and Other Barriers

It was now just over two and a half years since I had started karate, and already eight months had passed since the Japanese team had come and gone. I thought about the past nine months. I had participated in two gradings since being admitted into the black belt club, and I was now first *kyu*. My next step was the coveted belt that every *karateka* strives for and dreams about, first *dan* black belt.

The *kyu* grades from eighth *kyu* up to first *kyu* are known as student grades. First *dan* is the first rung on the ladder of master grades, with the supreme level (to date) being 10th *dan*--a grade with which a small number of masters have been honored in Japan.

My other friends were all training together with me again, but only Lucas, Mannie, and I had been invited by the leaders of our *dojo* to enter the gradings. Unlike the *kyu* gradings, which were conducted on a local or provincial scale, the *dan* gradings were on a national level. I had heard from many people that this was a stiff test with an average pass rate of only 50 percent. Unsuccessful candidates were told they could try again after six months. The *dan* gradings were held bi-annually. The testing panel was called the *shihankai*, comprised of seven or eight senior adjudicators who held the level of fifth *dan* or above.

I was told that it took approximately 17 years of intensive training and study to reach fifth *dan* level, and very few achieved this. Most of the panel had taken their higher *dan* grade in Japan.

I was deeply interested when Mike explained how the time period between gradings and examinations grew longer as the *dan* levels became higher. The student had about three or four months waiting period between each of the *kyu* levels, but the time between first and second *dan* was an average of about two years.

Between second and third *dan*, the *karateka* had to wait three years, and so on. If one carried a sixth *dan*, the waiting period before seventh *dan* would be approximately seven years from the time sixth *dan* was awarded.

If one were a full-time trainee in Japan within the instructor training system, promotions to higher levels might be speeded up somewhat, but not to a great extent. It was a long process of self-development, striving, and growth.

The initial task is the development and conditioning of the body through the *kyu* levels. Then comes the learning of strategies at first and second *dan* levels. In the third *dan* realm one has to be able to effectively apply the techniques and strategies that one has learned from one's teachers and colleagues. Fourth and fifth *dan* stages herald the birth of the apprentice master. He begins to develop his own strategies. His unique artistry begins to emerge. He is able to creatively express his own art to the full.

At sixth *dan* level and above, the young master of the technical side of karate begins to change and mature. He starts to consider, explore, and research *karate-do* as it relates to life. In other words, his task is to develop into a true master or *shihan*, skillful technician, teacher, wise leader and friend, a real exponent of the broad concept of self-defense---one who is not only going through the process of conquering himself, but who is sincere and skillful in helping his fellow beings to conquer their weaknesses in body, mind, and spirit, and thus helping them to approach an understanding of what true self-defense is.

The syllabus for black belt grading is very similar to the brown belt requirements. Brown belt is, in fact a preparation for black belt. Repetition and more repetition is the key to the black belt training. The *sensei* insisted that I do between 10 and 20 *Bassai Dai katas* every day, and this *kata* has 47 moves. The same applies to *kihon* and *kumite*. We would often move up and down the *dojo* doing combinations of blocks, kicks, and strikes for one hour at a time. "Your moves must begin to exist in you," urged the *sensei*.

Lucas and I put in extra training time whenever we could. On the weekends, I would visit his home where we stretched, kicked at a sandbag, and punched a *makiwara* that he had roped to a tree. There was great rivalry between the two of us. We would always try to outdo each other at sit-ups, press-ups, chinning bar, and squat kicks. If we went on a run, the final 200 or 300 meters was a race to see who could get back to the gate first. We shared the wins and losses.

We couldn't resist doing free fighting against each other, even though it was not a requirement for the first *dan* level. Our *kumite* was very rough, and we often came out nursing bruises, sore fingers, toes, and the occasional swollen lip. Our free fighting struggle sometimes ended in a clinch. We would then try to trip each other and grapple on the lawn, often rolling into the flower beds. One Saturday afternoon our training ceased promptly when we both rolled onto a well-camouflaged prickly pear leaf and became instantly airborne.

Once, after an indecisive argument on how powerful our punches and strikes were, we decided to test them by breaking wood and tiles. The *sensei* had warned us that breaking techniques could be harmful if one' approach was incorrect or if the limbs had not been properly conditioned. We paid a visit to the local hardware store and purchased various lengths of wood and some concrete roofing tiles.

"This is an unusual order," remarked the attendant. "What are you fellows going to do with this stuff?"

"Break it," replied Lucas, to which I added, "or rather, try to break it."

"You're kidding!" He looked at us incredulously. "What for?"

Lucas and I glanced at each other. I noticed a number of customers had become interested. We felt like kicking ourselves for having said anything. Lucas and I with full arms and peeping over the top, started for the exit.

"Well?" called the attendant.

"It's for a karate demonstration," I lied, edging towards the door. Now all of the customers were gazing directly towards us.

"That's interesting. Where is it being held?" inquired the attendant.

"In my back yard," replied Lucas. We beat a hasty retreat.

On the way back to Lucas' home, we passed Stephen's apartment.

"We are going to have a try at some tiles and wood. Do you think you could spare some time to show us?" we asked.

"Go on ahead; I'll come to your place shortly," he agreed.

Before he arrived we tried our hand out on a plank. It was only about one centimeter thick and about 60 centimeters long. We allowed the edges to rest on two stools, and I tried *shuto uchi*.* All that happened was that my hand bounced off the wood each time. Lucas had a few tries and didn't fare any better.

"Having trouble?" We turned. Stephen was chuckling. "That's mahogany, far too springy. Try one of those pine boards, rather." The boards were about 45 centimeters by 30 centimeters and approximately two and a half centimeters thick. He showed Lucas how to hold the board, cushioning it against ;the heels of his hands with his elbows wedged in to keep it firm. "Hold it about stomach height," he told Lucas. Then he told me to tap it lightly with a reverse punch, getting the correct line, stance, and distance. "Rotate your hips and keep your elbows in. Tense and breathe out sharply as you make contact. Go ahead!"

I did as he said, and the wood snapped on impact.

"Good!" he exclaimed.

Lucas also succeeded. "Are your fists not sore?" inquired Stephen.

"Fine!" we exclaimed, amazed at how easily the wood had broken. "Could we try two planks?" asked Lucas.

"Let me look at your hands." asked Stephen. "Ah, I can see that you ;have both been doing a lot of *makiwara* work. Your knuckles are in strong condition, but remember the *sensei* does not like us to do too much of this breaking technique. If it is done only occasionally as a test of one's skill, it is not too serious. Try two planks if you like, but remember, if they don't break, you can hurt your fist."

---

* *shuto uchi*—knife-hand strike

I held the two planks while Lucas positioned himself. He measured his distance and struck; nothing happened. Stephen assisted me in holding the two boards more securely. "Try again; take your time." Lucas tried--a thud--but the planks were still intact.

"Rather leave it. How's your fist?" asked Stephen.

"My fist is okay, but my wrist is slightly sore. It buckled over as I hit," he said.

"You need more *makiwara* work," said Stephen.

I also tried two planks, but did not succeed. My fist was not hurt, but then Stephen pointed out that I did not give it all I had. I guess I was still a bit wary.

"Let me have a try," said Stephen, "but make sure that you hold the planks squarely to the front, and don't allow any give as I make contact." We gripped the planks tightly. He assumed a forward stance with his hips turned out 45 degrees, then smoothly rotated his towards the wood and aimed his fist to its center. He did this a number of times, breathing out as he reached the target each time. His hips and body seemed to advance forwards as the punch softly touched the wood center and moved backwards as he wound up for the next test aim. As he gently completed the third test, there was a sudden whirl of action, a sharp *kiai*, and the two boards broke in half. We were amazed.

"How did you do that, *Sempai*? I asked.

"Faith," he answered, smiling.

He gave us an interesting explanation of the importance of *kime* in the martial arts. "Your mind, body, and spirit must be totally behind your blow,": he said. "In his book on martial arts, Michel Random tells us that the mind controls the body and that *ki* is the energy that affects the union between mind and body. *ki* is like original vital energy. The *karateka* generates *ki* from his lower abdomen and transmits it via his hips. Energy, believe the martial artists, is neither good nor bad. It is what the mind and conscience make of it. If the mind is positive, the energy itself will become positive and creative. A bad, negative mind, will similarly develop a negative energy. If one shouts from the depths of the abdomen, the energy output will be increased. Strong vibration is generated.

kime is the gathering of all the body's physical and psychological forces. *kime* has a power of penetration. Although the blow stops short, the *kime* continues, like a laser beam."

"How do we learn to generate this *ki*?" I asked.

"By more and more dedicated karate training," replied Stephen. "I am still a novice when it comes to *ki*. Try the tiles now," he urged. "First do one, then two, and so on, building up your confidence, and most important, pad them with a bath towel to avoid injury."

He showed us how to span ;the tiles across two separated bricks. By the end of the afternoon, we were able to break a pile of seven roof tiles without hurting our fists.

As I drove home that evening, I had mixed feelings. On the one hand, I felt that I had a long way to go to harness the better part of my potential. On the other hand, the tile breaking had given me confidence. Before, I was not quite sure of how effective my blows would be if I had to use them in a real situation. Now, I knew that my punch had come "oomph" behind it--not yet as much as Stephen's--but I resolved I would keep training hard. His power impressed me.

Chapter 9

Entering the Black Belt Realm

As I advanced in the general class and became a senior purple belt, I felt a sense of responsibility towards the lower-graded members of my class. My seniority had given me a feeling of importance. Like a junior high school prefect, I had moved to high school—the black belt club. For the past nine months, I had existed much like a small fish in a big pond. That important purple belt was now a very unimportant brown belt, I had begun to feel.

My body was stiff from the training, and I had lost too much weight. I felt worse than a novice. I concluded that I was the most unnoticed member of the class.

When my spirit was at its lowest ebb, an unexpected change took place. I and four other first *kyu* brown belts, who included Lucas, suddenly became the center of attraction. Where previously I felt that the *sensei* and the other seniors were studiously ignoring me, I now almost wished that they would.

Every move I made was exposed to a host of critical eyes. "Press your hips forward, bend your back knee more...still more...speed...more spirit...try it again...pull that fist back...again...harder, harder...get lower...keep your eyes up...back straight...that knee again, bend it more, turn the toe in...don't hold your breath...breathe with the blow...relax, only tense when you need to...not all the time...more *kime*...*kiai* louder...relax...don't be so tense!"

"*Osu!*" I would shout with much aggression. This was a different *osu* to the one I had used before. It was my only way at getting back at these merciless slave drivers. Nothing our group did was good enough. If we weren't being made to do a move a thousand times over, we were herded to the head of the class, still panting, and there we were made to face a queue of fresh black belts who took turns in trying out their *tokui waza** on us.

Again, the relentless coaching and criticism: "Block that...don't let him hit you...look up...that counter was too slow...move forwards, not backwards!" My forearm was swollen from blocking John's and Stephen's front kicks. I had been winded by John once and decided that a sore forearm was a better proposition than rolling around on the floor, struggling to get air into a par of deflated lungs.

The thunderclouds building up within me reached their darkest one night, when I felt as if every member of the class was out to eat me alive, including my friend, Lucas. I had been caught off guard four or five times and was not faring well. Suddenly I was hit on the nose, just hard enough to bring a few tears to my eyes. Something snapped within me; a spiritual metamorphosis took place. I discarded my sheep's clothing and became a wolf. I moved forward against the current, looking through my opponents without seeing them...doing what I needed to do...and then, the one ray of sunlight within the storm: "Good, very good!" spoken by the *sensei*. "You have made a breakthrough."

There were over 100 candidates lined up in the huge examination hall. A silence descended upon the large crowd of onlookers as the chief examiner Addressed us. He was flanked by six members of the *shihankai*.

"You will be judged by three independent sets of examiners." He pointed to a table at the far end of the hall. "You will do your *kihon* movements over there, then proceed to the next table where you will be tested for *kata*. At this table, you will do the *jiyu ippon kumite*.

"Black belt is a big step. Both physical factors as well as psychological factors will be taken into account. Firstly, in the *kihon*, your technique must be correct, powerful, and fast. In the *kata*, not only should you demonstrate good technique, but your movements

---

* *tokui waza* —favorite technique

should be an artful expression of defense against imaginary opponents. During the *kumite*, your attitude is of prime importance. Your aim should be to overcome your opponent through the use of strategy, good technique, and fighting spirit. But remember what Master Gichin Funakoshi always said: 'The art of karate is lost without etiquette and respect for others.' In other words, be hard on your opponent, but be a fair sportsman. Stick to the rules."

The grading followed the same format as the area gradings. After completing each of the sections without any serious mishap, I felt grateful to the *sensei* and my seniors for preparing me so thoroughly. As I walked off the area, I saw Mike give me the thumbs up sign from where he sat in the audience. What would the verdict be? The grading itself had not been all that bad. The tough part had been the buildup and, of course, the usual tension and anxiety the night before. Whether or not I had passed, I would know within the next hour. What concerned me now was something different. If I had passed, then the coming Monday night held for me a test more severe than I had ever faced—initiation into my own *dojo's* black belt club.

The last two graders completed their *kumite* and were told to line up. On the table were two stacks of examination cards, the passes and the fails. Our association secretary picked up one of the stacks and began reading out the names of the successful candidates. As each successful candidate was called, they stepped forward and bowed. Mannie's name was called. The stack was getting smaller and smaller. I felt my heart racing, and it leapt as Lucas' name was called out. There were about three cards left. My knees felt weak. As the thought crossed my mind that I may not have made it, my name was called.

In the change room, there was much jubilance from many of those who had passed. Some already had new black belts tied around their waists. Lucas and I congratulated the others but refused an invitation to join them at a nearby restaurant. We were in no mood for celebration with Monday night's initiation hanging over us.

It was a tradition at our *dojo* that successful graders appear at the Monday evening class still wearing brown belts. We would then have to fight every black belt in the class and undergo a special ceremony before being accepted into the black belt club.

What worried me most over the next two days was not the thought that I may be injured. I was more concerned whether or not I would last the distance. Other black belts had told me that they had never experienced anything as exhausting as the initiation.

After the Monday general class, the *sensei* asked all members below black belt to leave the *dojo* as soon as they had showered and changed. Lucas, Mannie, and I waited in the foyer of the *dojo*. The other black belts didn't tarry to talk to us.

The *sensei* summoned us to line up, and I sensed the prevailing atmosphere. These black belts were serious. We would have to fight for the right of entering their domain.

The black belts formed a circle. I don't remember how many I fought. All I remember was a fusillade of blows coming incessantly at me, picking myself off the ground and trying to block the well-placed kicks and strikes, grappling and rolling around wildly on the ground again, which left me gasping for breath as I was raised to my feet and told to stand up to the next opponent, and the next, and so on.

All the time, the group pushed and encouraged me. By about my seventh fight, I could hardly get up from the floor, I was so tired from trying to prevent them from penetrating my faltering defenses. Mike hoisted me up and shouted, "Go harder, don't give in!" A new spirit overtook the old, and I overwhelmed my opponent with a barrage of blows that at first were telling, but as my energy waned, he seized the opportunity and swept both my feet off the floor. Landing on the wooden floor with a thud, I felt no physical pain—only a sense of inner panic at my unbearable sense of tiredness. The voices, "Get up, more spirit, you can do it!" It was like some terrible nightmare. I tried to will my limbs to act, but they seemed to move in slow motion.

"Never give in...last fight...fight for your life!"

The *sensei's* voice cut through the shroud of oblivion that seemed to be smothering my very soul. My entire being responded to the *sensei's* call. I felt goose pimples covering my body as a new psychic energy refueled me. Standing firm, I blocked off every blow that my assailant threw at me, and as he paused to gather breath, my left leg instinctively shot out scoring an *ippon**** to his head.

"*Yame!*" ordered the *sensei*. Hardly knowing what was happening, I was led to the nearby wall and told to sit and meditate.

It was now Lucas' turn. My back was turned to the activity, yet the familiar noises were resonating distantly in my floating mind, echoing across what seemed to be a long tunnel of space...a protracted *dojo*...comprising endless sounds.

Lucas' ordeal was over as was Mannie's and the three of us now sat facing the row of black belts. The *sensei* rose, approached me, and ordered me to stand up. I bowed to him. He unfastened his own black belt and tied it around my waist, over my brown belt. He bowed to me and returned to his position. A similar ritual was performed on the others.

Each of the seniors spoke to us like wise older brothers. We were praised for our spirit of fortitude, yet reminded that we were now expected to be living examples of *karate-do* both in and out of the *dojo*. Finally, the *sensei* spoke: "You have earned your black belt; don't hang it up in your cupboard. Wear it every day, and you will begin to discover the potential that you possess." He paused and with a warmth that was indescribable said, "We welcome you to our black belt fraternity. Remember, this is only the beginning."

The black belts had arranged a special party in our honor, which we celebrated at a nearby restaurant. It was through functions such as this that we came to know them as human beings. They were from different walks of life and a diverse mixture of age and ethnic groups, yet we were able to relate to one another in an empathetic fashion. If one had a problem, there was always someone willing to

---

* *ippon*—full point

help. As harsh as we were with one another on the floor, the opposite was true off the floor. Late one night my car was stuck. I could not contact my family, so I telephoned Mike. Within minutes he arrived and cheerfully hitched my car to the back of his and towed me home. I was moved by his helpful attitude. When I handed him a small gift the next evening, he said, "Thanks, but that's not necessary. We are karate men. The best gift is for you to be hard on me on the floor."

Chapter 10

At the Crossroads—A Choice of Alternatives

The initial excitement of wearing the black belt had hardly worn off when the *sensei* called me into his office. "I would like to discuss your future development," he said. " remember you telling me that you would someday like to train in Japan. Is that right?"

"Yes, *sensei*," I replied.

"Well, that is interesting. You know that once a *karateka* reaches first *dan*, he has a number of choices ahead of him. There are three main alternatives. Firstly, if he does not desire to become a karate champion or instructor, he can continue training in the classes of his choice, maintaining his fitness and continuing to develop his skills. Without exceptional pressures upon him, he can reach the level of second *dan*. Secondly, he may desire to enter into the karate tournaments and gain local and national colors either in the spheres of participation or judging. This requires extra effort, and more pressure is placed upon him. The third alternative follows from the second, and that is aiming at becoming a qualified instructor. The pressures are even greater. It means a very severe test at third *dan* level. The third *dan* test is a necessary step in the process of becoming a qualified instructor."

My eyes were riveted upon the *sensei* as he talked. Then he stopped and looked directly at me without saying anything.

"*Sensei*," I returned, "what do you think I should do?"

"I don't think," smiled the *sensei*. "I only do what is necessary." Calmly, he waited.

"I want to go all the way," I blurted out.

"All right, now I know what to do," he nodded. The interview instantly ended.

Having achieved first *dan*, I felt a new sense of strength. I remembered something Stephen had said, which I was only now beginning to understand. He said that it took about a year after having been graded to feel truly worthy of one's level. "How true," I reflected. It was almost a year since that big day. My other friends, Nick, Lisa, and Jack, had recently received their black belts. From the white belt class of 30, only six had finally achieved black belt level. It was something of a record, I believe, because our association secretary told me that, on average, less than 5 percent of those who take up karate ever reach black belt first *dan*.

There was a minimum waiting period of two years between first and second *dan*. The past year had been extremely interesting for me. In training for second *dan*, the main tasks are to further improve and strengthen one's techniques. Then comes the task of mastering the ever-changing combinations of these techniques. Creativity is blended with mechanics.

In addition to *Bassai Dai kata*, which I had done for *shodan* and would again do for *nidan*, I was now expected to learn and practice four additional *katas—Kanku Dai, Hangetsu, Empi,* and *Jion.*

Each of these *kata* had a different character. It is like getting to know a new friend, a friend who possesses qualities that one does not possess and thus by continual interaction with a new *kata*, new problems are confronted and understood. Each time one conquers a problem, a new understanding of one's self begins to emerge. My own *kata, Bassai Dai,* is an earthy, powerful *kata* characteristic of concentrated force and may be compared to the idea of a battering ram penetrating a castle stronghold.

Kanku Dai is a long and demanding *kata*. It consists of 62 moves. When first teaching it to us, the *sensei* mentioned that *Kanku Dai* is considered to be one of the primary *katas* by most JKA masters. "Going through *Kanku Dai* is like going through life," he said. The *kata* opens with arms and hands describing a great, smooth outward circle like someone describing their future aims. It ends with a great incircling of the hands and arms, implying that the outward adventures have led to inward spiritual understanding. The *kata* itself requires one to move in all directions—characteristic of the ups and downs of life. The aim is to complete the *kata* in even greater spirit than that with which one started, like the courageous marathon runner who, despite physical hardships and pain, transcends the physical and sprints the last straight with nothing but fighting spirit drawing him to victory.

Hangetsu is a *kata* of opposites—slow, crescent-shaped moves suddenly contrasted with quick, fiery, linear moves. It is aptly named half moon, for its introspective nature is aimed at the building of inner strength.

By contrast, *Empi* is a light, fast, happy, outward-energy kata. The joyful changing flight of the swallow is the personality of *Empi*.

Jion is, in a way, a return to basic elements. Like *Bassai Dai*, it is a strong *kata*, yet it demands subtlety of expression that can be enhanced by first having become acquainted with the other *katas*.

After a stimulating session in which we practiced these five *katas*, the *sensei* spoke to us. "*Kata*, as you all know, is a series of moves against imaginary opponents. A phrase from the *samurai* creed illuminates this idea: 'I have no enemy; I make incautiousness my enemy.' There are imaginary opponents that surround us and those that are within us. If we were to examine ourselves, would we not discover that we often see opponents that, in reality, do not exist and are only illusions?"

Nick looked absorbed and almost unconsciously answered, "Yes, *Sensei*, that is really true."

The *sensei* invited him to give an example. "Well," he said, "until recently, I always felt inferior to most people. Maybe it is because I am a foreigner in this country. It is only now that I can see that this was my imaginary opponent, and it took me all these years to realize that I do possess some good qualities."

"Nick," said the *sensei*, smiling, "I am very happy you have made this breakthrough. Many people go through life wrestling themselves into the dust, never winning. It is quite obvious that you have a deeper understanding of what is meant by imaginary opponents. *Karate-do* consists of peeling away certain barriers that prevent us from clearly seeing the truth of our lives.

"Ten years ago, while in Japan, I was unsuccessfully struggling to do leg splits. An instructor approached me and asked what I was doing. 'My legs are very stiff,' I said to him. His rejoinder was an all-time classic: 'Oh, really, you say you have stiff legs. I say maybe you have stiff mind.'

"It took me years to realize how right he was. I had created my own imaginary opponent—stiffness. My mind was filled with stiffness, and it was always my favorite excuse. Now I am learning to fill my mind, instead, with ways of getting supple. Maybe I will learn how to empty it someday.

"Is it important for the *karateka* to understand power, speed, agility, aggression, calmness, et cetera?"

"Of course," we agreed.

"The ideal *kata* contains each of these elements and many more. The art is to be able to become the tidal wave, and the next instant, if necessary, the flash of lightning—to have the all-seeing eye of the eagle. If we have to cope with aggression, we need to become aggression, like the tigress' spirit when her cubs are threatened. We also need to become the calmness of the quiet desert night. Through *kata* we can become living examples of these ideas, the ultimate being self-control. Our aim, therefore, is to become at one with our situation and to see it clearly, acting appropriately. To do this, we need to be able to communicate with our entire being. In other words, live in what you are trying to communicate. As Gichin Funakoshi implied, 'Become invincible and cope with 1,000 adversaries if in the cause of justice but, on the other hand, if you are wrong, apologize, making good your debt to even the weakest person.'

"Be invincible when it is time to be invincible, and when the time is right, be human. The secret lies in skill and timing. Learn and develop all the skills you can. Mostly refrain from using them, for this ability transcends skill. It is a rare, yet delicious fruit known as virtue."

I found that these infrequent talks given by the *sensei* were like a miracle tonic. I felt enthusiastic and could not wait for the next training session. I had begun to notice that the *sensei's* classes were not all hard and physically demanding. Often he would relax the pace for a few days and concentrate more on form and learning.

It was mostly during these light periods that he would talk to us, rekindling our sometimes over-tempered spirits.

There were times when I really felt low, as if I was getting nowhere. Some would call this staleness. The *sensei* would pull me out of this state by changing his approach, and in a very short time, he would have me in a state where I was all but begging him to give the class the harder training again.

"We all move through plateaus of learning," he once told us. "At a certain point in your training you may feel satisfied, but often a new sense of inadequacy overcomes the self, and depression can be the result. This happens to all top athletes and artists." He elaborated further that the mind is quick to perceive a new idea. It thus jumps up ahead of the body to a higher level of understanding. Then one struggles to get the body to achieve this new idea. The body endeavors to master the new technique, so we experience frustration. If we eventually achieve it or get close, we experience a short-lived satisfaction, but invariably the mind once more grasps a fresh concept, and the whole process of struggle begins again. "This," he told us, "is the suffering that every developing *karateka* must accept if he desires to grow and keep improving. It is an unending quest for recognition and recreation. It is the sacrifice he makes for the gift he will receive."

I was just becoming accustomed to feeling somewhat more serene and secure when the *sensei* sprang two new surprises on me.

"Would you be able to teach once a week? It will be one or two beginners at first."

I was pleased and honored that he had chosen me.

"You will be helping both me and yourself," he pointed out. "Another thing, I have been watching your free fighting. We have decided to include you in our *dojo* A team at the national championships."

I was flabbergasted and started to protest: "But there are others who are better..." Before I could finish, the *sensei* cut in with, "You have been chosen!"

The teaching was not easy. I was given six new white belt beginners. They were a complete mixture of ages. I would demonstrate a technique and ask the class to do it. The two children in the class were distracted by the activities in the *dojo* and did everything except what I asked, while the others performed a half-baked version of the techniques. I felt a twinge of uneasiness as I realized that I was not getting through to them. My approach was wrong, I realized. I was expecting too much, too soon. Changing my approach, I explained how each basic technique was like a different weapon that had to be developed and strengthened. I then demonstrated against one of them showing how various blocks and attacks could be used in real-life situations. Immediately I noticed a change in the class. They did not take their eyes off me. Breaking down each technique into specific elements, I had the class repeat each separate part, gradually putting the parts together until they were doing a complete technique. I adopted this approach with each technique. As soon as they did the technique reasonably well, I had them do target training. For example, with a stepping punch, I had the class aim their technique at various parts of the anatomy of their partners, pulling it just short of contact. The next step was for the partners to learn how to block each of these blows.

As the weeks passed, I developed better ways of training my small class. By instructing these people, I became extremely aware of my own strengths and limitations. Whatever weaknesses I had began to manifest themselves in my students. At one time, I kept telling the class to bend their back knee over their big toe. I would demonstrate the technique, but still the class didn't improve. Then the truth struck me. With childish innocence, the youngest boy said, "But *Sempai*, you don't have your back knee over your toe!"

Chapter 11

A Nest Full of Challenges

At first, training for the championships was very similar to normal training except that we did a great deal of *makiwara* hitting and bag kicking as well.

"Your bodies are now solid, and your techniques are strong. You're ready to go into specific championship training," said the *sensei.* "This will mainly consist of reflex drills, target training on a moving target, development of a favorite technique with which you train to penetrate your opponent under varying circumstances, and above, we will do actual matches according to tournament regulations. Today, you will do an extra match. Tomorrow it will be two matches, the next day three, and so on. We will build up to approximately 10 matches per day and then taper off again. Each of you will take turns in acting as center referee as well as being one of the four side judges. It is important that all contestants are fully acquainted with the rules. You will be taught as you go along. By the end of three weeks, you should be well conditioned into tournament procedure."

The first week of training was confusion for me...from training and sweating...to judging and making mistake after mistake....having to compete against the other black belts. I did not win many matches. My mind was filled with a lot of new terms and conditions. I was confused further by the incessant changing of roles from student to judge to participant. Each of these required the utmost concentration of mind, body, and spirit.

The matches were governed by a center referee who was assisted by four side judges, each of whom sat at one corner of the taped, eight meter square fighting area. Each had a whistle in his mouth, a red flag in one hand, and a white flag in the other. The two contestants, the one with a red tag on his belt and the other with a white tag, would bow before entering the fighting area and then, summoned by the center referee, they would take up their starting positions on the two lines, three meter apart, in the center of the fighting area.

On the command, "*Hajime*," the protagonists would advance on one another, each endeavoring to penetrate the opponent's defenses, trying to score an *ippon*, which means full point or killing blow.

In our practice contests, very few *ippons* were awarded. If one scored *ippon*, the match was over.

"*Ippon*," explained the *sensei*, "is perfection personified. It has to be a powerful and superb technique executed correctly and accurately to one of the opponent's vulnerable areas, such as face or stomach, and pulled just short of contact. The perfect *ippon* occurs when, as a result of clever strategy and timing, the opponent is caught at an unguarded moment. This is the aim of contest, to overcome one's opponent by seeking *kyo*, or creating *kyo*, and finally attacking *kyo*."

Kyo is a difficult term to translate. It basically means, "good timing." Another way of looking at *kyo* is to see *kyo* as weakness. In other words, to seek weakness in the opponent, or to create weakness in him and finally to attack his weakness.

On the seventh day of training, John, wearing a read tag, faced Lucas. Lucas feinted with a kick, but unexpectedly followed through with a stepping punch to the abdomen. Three side judges blew their whistles, holding their white flags out horizontally. The other judge crossed his flags in front of his eyes, indicating that he was unsighted. Mike, the center referee, shouted, "*Yame!*" and ordered the contestants back to their starting lines. He announced "*Shiro chudan zuki*,"* then extending his arm smartly downwards in Lucas' direction, he said, "*Waza-ari*," which meant that Lucas had scored an effective technique or half point. It was good, but not quite good enough for *ippon*.

---

* *shiro chudan zuki*—white, mid-level punch

John looked calm. Lucas could not wait to get going. Before Mike could call *tsuzukete hajime*,[*] Lucas was already moving forwards off his starting line. "*Yame*," shouted Mike. "*Motonoichi*,"[*] he admonished.

The match restarted with Lucas the aggressor. It became evident that John was about to maneuver Lucas into an uncompromising position. Lucas repeated his kick feint, stepped forwards, but as his foot was about to touch the floor, John changed from a forward stance into a back stance, hooked his front foot around Lucas' unstable ankle causing him to lift off the floor with his head whirling towards John's superbly timed close punch. John's confident *kiai* was echoed by a shrill blast of whistles, and his ippon was confirmed by four vertical red flags.

Mike announced, "*Aka jodan zuki ippon*."[*] This time he extended his arm upwards in the direction of John, the winner.

Quite unmoved, John bowed and moved off the area. Lucas, on the other hand, although physically unharmed, was shaking his head in disbelief, still unable to comprehend John's shock tactic.

With each successive day, the pressure was increased. The championships would consist of both *kata* and *kumite* contests. The stressful demands of this intensive training had marked effects on certain members of the team. The daily competition had caused frustration among some. When the training had first started, Lucas had beaten me a number of times, but in our last three confrontations, I had won. I now sensed an edginess about him as we faced each other again.

The command, *hajime*, had hardly passed Stephen's lips when Lucas attacked me. The combination of kicks and punches had me back-pedaling, but his third technique, a powerful front kick, broke through my guard, and he was awarded a half point. As he rushed me a second time, I dropped low, deflecting his face punch and

---

[*] *tsuzukete hajime*—a command to continue fighting

[*] *motonoichi*—a command to return to the starting line

[*] *aka jodan zuki ippon*—red, face punch, full point

scoring a half point with a stomach punch. It was match point, and I could tell that he was determined to score. He tried to distract my attention by pretending to do his favorite right front kick, but suddenly he switched to a left front kick. I simultaneously released a roundhouse kick to his head. Both our blows were well placed.

"*Yame*," shouted Stephen. "*Ai-uchi*." He pointed his fists towards each other at chest level, signifying that we had scored simultaneously. Our points position remained unchanged.

As we resumed the match, Lucas rushed forward, his fists and legs flying. I moved backwards, and my right foot stepped out of the area. The referee shouted, "*Yame!*" I stopped, but Lucas had not heard it. His right fist caught the side of my nose, and within seconds, blood was running down my face, discoloring my *gi*. The four side judges were blowing their whistles loudly, and frantically rotating their white flags above their heads. This meant that Lucas, wearing a white tag, had committed *hansoku*.[*]

Stephen called us to our starting positions and disqualified Lucas for excessive contact. Lucas' apology did not alter my contained anger. I was out to repay him in our next confrontation. The healthy rivalry between us had, it seemed, become marred by an ugly undertone. I wrestled with my feelings, but nothing could dissuade me from revenge. He was getting too big for his boots.

Self-control was one of the maxims, I reflected, but I superimposed against these words a phrase I had read in the Bible, "...eye for eye..."

The *sensei* must have sensed the silent antagonism between us, because he did not match us again. In any case, he began to reduce the pace, giving us a lighter form of training.

"In these last few days, the aim is a rebuilding of energy. By the time the big day comes, you will all be aching to get on to that floor. You will be in prime condition."

"Well," I thought, "in that case, I'll just have to wait. Lucas needs a lesson."

---

[*] *hansoku*—disqualification due to a serious infringement

Over the next few days, I tried to forget the incident with Lucas, but my tender nose remained a nagging reminder. One evening, as I was driving home, my mind over-filled with Lucas, I unconsciously cut across into another lane of traffic, quite unaware that I had narrowly missed a car that was about to overtake me.

A blaring hooter and a gesticulating driver told me something was wrong. He overtook me, edged me on to the side of the road and leapt out of his car. I wasn't going to be caught sitting. We met at the bonnet of my car. He was red in the face, ranting and raving and slapping my car with his open hands, shouting what an idiot I was and how I had nearly killed him. I was taken by surprise. In a garbled voice I apologized, but this seemed only to add fuel to the blazing fire. He moved closer and unleashed a string of abuse at me. His breath smelled of alcohol, and I was dominated by his focused anger and didn't like what I felt inside.

Then he took a wild swing at my face. Without realizing it, my arm short-circuited the blow.

"I already told you I was sorry," I said to him, now looking directly into his eyes. I must have captured some of his spirit, for he now moved back a pace, wagged his finger at me telling me that I had better "watch it." I just stood and looked. He shook his head, turned, and stomped off to his car.

I got back into my car and felt shaky as I drove along the familiar highway. I did not like the feeling that this unpleasant incident had evoked within me. It was the unhappy mixture of failure and inadequacy. I reasoned that the incident had probably worked out for the best, but I was unable to rationalize the sick feeling in my stomach. Amid these conflicting thoughts, I found myself driving back towards the *dojo*. I had to speak to someone. I must see the *sensei*. As I arrived at the *dojo*, the *sensei* was about to leave.

"What's the problem?" he asked, sensing that I was not my normal self.

"I don't know if I should be bothering you, but something is worrying me," I told him.

He set his bag down, eased himself against the mud guard of his car, and motioned me to speak. I described what had happened on the way home and how I felt about it.

"Well," he asked, "if you are not happy about what you did, what, then, do you think you should have done instead?"

"Well, it is not so much what I did that worries me," I told him. "It was more the feeling of being dominated that worried me. I felt insecure. I would like to have felt controlled and confident, like you teach us to be."

"Before we go on, do you think the other man was justified in saying that you nearly caused a serious accident?" He waited for my answer.

"I guess so," I answered. "But was it necessary for him to be so uncouth and..."

"Wait!" interrupted the *sensei*. "Never mind how the man spoke to you. What is important is that in the first instance you were wrong, correct?"

"Yes," I conceded.

"It's all very simple," explained the *sensei*. "The fact that you were wrong caused you to have a negative spirit. This is a natural feeling in any fair-minded human being. If, on the other hand, the man had not accepted your apology and began battering your car with a hammer, he then would have become the faulty party, and I have no doubt that your negative feelings would have become positive. Remember one thing: the cause must be right before the spirit can be right."

I nodded, slowly beginning to half understand this idea. Then he asked the question that focused in on the real truth of the matter.

"Why were you unaware of that other car when you cut him off?" he probed.

It was as if he had hit me hard between the eyes. Of course, I had been unaware of my immediate environment only because I could not get Lucas out of my mind. I told the *sensei* the whole story. He touched my shoulder reassuringly. "It is human nature to blame others when we get hurt. I have done it all too often myself only to realize my folly later. Many years ago, I went with a similar problem to my Japanese master, and he told me a little story"

"Two monks were strolling down a sand road when they came upon a wide, muddy patch. A young, lovely lady, dressed in a gaily colored *kimono* with clean, white stockings and bamboo sandals stood looking at the mud, perplexed. As the monks approached, she spoke to one of them, asking, 'Dear sir, I am going to a wedding. How do you think I can cross without getting mud all over me?'

"'How would I know?' mumbled the monk, who moved past her and crossed the muddy surface. The second monk went straight up to her, picked her up in his arms, carried her across, put her down, and bade her farewell.

"For seven miles, the two monks walked along in silence. Suddenly, the first monk stopped, faced the other, and in an accusing voice said, 'Brother, you did an unforgivable thing. You know that we are not supposed to consort with females. How could you have picked up that woman?'

"The second monk smiled, looking directly into the other's eyes, and quietly answered, 'Brother, I put her down seven miles ago. Are you still carrying her?'"

We laughed. I felt spiritually freed.

* * *

People were streaming into the hall as our team bus arrived at the championship venue. This was the annual JKA (Japan Karate Association) style championship, and karate athletes from all over the country would be competing.

Each team comprised seven members. Our *dojo* had been edged into second place the previous year, and we were all out to capture the crown this time.

In the first round, what should have been a walkover for us turned out to be a narrowly won contest. Our first two fighters, in their over-enthusiasm, made excessive contact, and we found ourselves two-nil down. Our number three went on and was defeated by the opposing captain, who had a great deal of international experience. We were three-nil down.

If we lost the next match, we would be out of the tournament as the system was on a knockout basis.

I was on fourth. As our coach, Mike, tied the red tag around my waist, he spoke quietly. "You've got to take this one."

I immediately put pressure on my opponent, who kept backing away from me and going out of the area. As I attacked, he moved away. At one point, as he continued going backwards, there was a sound of whistles and "*Yame*," from the referee. My opponent was throwing out wild punches, and one of the side judges thrust out his white flag indicating that my opponent had scored a *waza-ari*. The other three judges waved their flags across each other indicating that this was no point. The referee waved his hands across each other and announced, "*Tori-masen*."*

He explained that white had attempted to score while his foot was out of the area. This was not acceptable, and considering that this was the third time he had stepped out of the area, he was given *jogai, chui** by the referee. This was equivalent to my being awarded a *waza-ari*.

As the referee restarted the match, I immediately stepped in and scored a *waza-ari* with a straight punch to the face. The match was mine.

Lucas, John, and Stephen each won their matches, and we narrowly won by four matches to three.

There were now eight teams left for the second round. This proved to be a good round for us. A clean sweep of victory of seven-nil took us through to the third round. In the semi-finals, we were to meet a very strong team. My rival, Neville the goalie, was in this team. In this semi-final match, I was to go on second last

---

* *tori-masen*—no point
* *jogai, chui*—a warning for moving outside the prescribed fighting area

and Lucas last. John went on first and won easily with a back-fist strike.

By the fifth match, we were three-two up. I was in the sixth slot. By some strange act of fate, so was Neville. I had noticed in his other matches that he had become extremely agile, scoring a number of times with *mae tobi geri.** He leapt and bounced all over the place, and this was an intimidating tactic.

As Mike tied the white tag around me, he told me to keep cool, not move around too much, and watch for an opening. "Block. Use your fists against him," he advised. But his words seemed wasted on me.

Neville had set a bouncing rhythm, and I unconsciously followed suit. In other words, he was calling the tune, and I was dancing to it. All seemed to be going well when suddenly, after trying to do an acrobatic leap, I half slipped and like a missile, Neville flew at me as I was trying to regain balance, and his airborne left foot found my midriff. The crowd yelled. He had scored *waza-ari*.

Back on the starting line, my heart was beating too quickly. I had made the unforgivable mistake of fighting a man at his own game.

This time I rooted myself down and became the pivot point of the contest. He circled around me, moved up and down, in and out. I waited, edging gradually forwards, my arms ready to shoot out. Suddenly he leapt at me. My left fist exploded, and like a dead weight, Neville dropped to the floor. "*Yame!*" shouted the referee. A sense of panic gripped my chest. The doctor and the first aid crew rolled his inert form over. As they worked on him, I felt as though the whole world had fallen from under me. I had mistimed my blow and sent it on a collision course.

Neville was recovering. He shook his head and tried to sit up, but was told to relax while the doctor examined his eyes.

"A mild case of concussion," the doctor said. "No more fighting today for you."

---

* *mae tobi geri* — front flying kick

I was less worried about losing the match than what I had done to my rival and friend. I apologized to him profusely. He took it like the great sportsman that he was and blamed himself. I reflected and thought of my immature reaction when Lucas had touched my nose.

My lack of control had not done my team any good, for the points position was three matches all and one to go. The outcome now rested in Lucas' hands.

From the start of the match, I could see that Lucas would have tough opposition. His opponent was an aggressive individual who crouched and slugged in a boxing fashion. Although he missed with his first few swings, he blows were uncontrolled and dangerous, and he appeared unconcerned about stopping them. He would throw his fists forwards with his body following afterwards. He was thus unbalanced and a danger to Lucas. The referee cautioned him once, telling him not to deliver blows when he was off balance. Lucas' tactic was to keep a safe distance. Suddenly, he tried his favorite front kick. The slugger doubled-up, half smothering the kick with his arms and then with his eyes closed, he flung out a wild right hook just as Lucas penetrated with a stepping punch to his face. The slugger dropped to one knee, clutching his head. The referee rushed to examine the slugger, whose lip was slightly cut. None of the judges had noticed that Lucas had also taken a crack on the side of the head. He had not even flinched. He walked calmly back to his starting line and stood there, waiting.

We had been taught by our *sensei* that flinching was a sign of weakness. He had said, "If in a fight, whether tournament or other, you fail to block a blow and it makes contact, it should switch you on, not off. Those who flinch and stop to grasp the injured area have lost their spirit and given in. They are easy to beat in a real situation. You are practicing a fighting art. Act like a fighter. Never give in."

The side judges were rotating their white flags in a small circle above their heads. In response, the referee stepped backwards, pointed downward in Lucas' direction, and announced, "*Shiro,* *hansoku chui.*"* The match resumed. We were in a precarious position. If Lucas even touched his opponent lightly a second time, he would be disqualified. We held our breath as Lucas dodged the slugger's fists. I could see Lucas was planning something as he began to swing in a similar fashion towards the slugger's face—only his face. I had never seen him do this before, but I noticed that his blows were well controlled. I then realized he was trying to make his opponent lift his arms. The slugger was falling for the trick. More and more the action looked like a boxing match—all blows and parries. Lucas feinted with a right cross. The slugger responded by blocking upwards and to the left with both hands, exposing, for a moment, his stomach. Lucas' body suddenly reversed direction. Rotating in a clockwise direction, he released a superb back kick. It could not have been better timed, for the gong sounded the end of the match a second later. Lucas had taken us through to the finals.

Our opponents were the same team who had captured the title form us the year before—a formidable squad. This team had two members of the national team on their side, but we also had two national squad members, John and Stephen. Our team mounted the rostrum on the white side. As we bowed to our opponents, I wondered whom I would be fighting.

Wayne, the big fourth *dan* from the morning instructor's class, was the captain of this team. I was to go on fourth.

Before the beginning of each match, the coach and captain write the order of appearance on a sheet of paper, which is then handed to the officials. Thus, no one knew who would be meeting whom. I was silently praying that my opponent would not be Wayne.

John put us one up with the first match.

The second match we lost narrowly. The referee called time limit; each opponent had a *waza-ari*. The referee called for a judges' decision. There were two red flags and two white flags. The casting vote lay in the referee's hands. He could give a draw

---

* *shiro, hansoku chui*—white, a minor infringement

or award the match to the fighter who he felt was superior. His hand extended in the direction of the other team. We were one-all. Our third member had to face Wayne. The match was almost over before it started. Wayne pretended to start an attack. Our man flinched and move away. Wayne paused. Our man relaxed, and in that moment, Wayne whirled in with a reverse roundhouse kick. Four red flags shot upright, but before the referee could call, "*Yame*," Wayne's foot switched to a reverse leg sweep, scooping our man onto his back. The same foot continued to move in an upward arc, then descended again like a sharp guillotine cut to his opponent's midriff.

The crowd rose to their feet and cheered wildly. He had, in the space of one second, scored two *ippons*. The rules allow for only one to be awarded. It was more than sufficient to win him the match. His timing and control were superb. Our man had not a scratch on him. We were now one match down.

I was on next. My opponent was a powerful man, a good blocker. He stopped everything I threw at him in a most unorthodox way. He was all elbows and knees, and my left hand began aching after having made contact with his elbow instead of finding the target. The gong was sounded once, which meant that there were only 30 seconds left to go. Neither of us had scored. I moved in on him, gazing at his intent eyes, trying to create an opening. Suddenly, I heard his coach say, "Just keep away from him; there are only three seconds to go." For a moment, he half turned his head, and in that critical time lapse, my fist homed in to score a *waza-ari*. The next instant the gong sounded twice. The referee called for a judges' decision. Up went four white flags. I was awarded the match. It was two-all.

The next match ended in a draw. Lucas was our sixth man on. His timing was out, and he was quickly dispatched.

Stephen looked pale as he bowed to his opponent, also a top contest man and national squad member. We had won two matches and they three. We needed this match to equalize. In a hard-fought contest during which we held our breath, Stephen managed to narrowly capture a half point lead as the final gong was sounded.

Each team had won and lost an equal number of matches. The captains were called to the officials' table. the final decision rested on which team had scored the most *ippons* and *waza-aris*. We waited tensely. The hall went silent as the chief referee prepared to announce the points decision.

"Red side scored a total of one *ippon* and three *waza-aris*." A pause. I was frantically hoping that we had scored more. He studied the paper before him and went on, "White side scored one *ippon* and three *waza-aris*." There was a buzz from the audience. "An equal points position," he announced. "Each team will now select one fighter for a final playoff."

John was our man and, of course, Wayne was theirs. It was to be a two-minute match. As they approached their starting lines, the audience rose to their feet and began applauding. This was the first time I had ever seen this. Goose pimples spread across my body.

Two years ago they had met in the finals of our national individual championships. Wayne had won. The audience sat down, but the cheering continued as the referee called, "*Hajime.*"

The applause seemed to be a catalyst for action. It was largely a contest of hands versus feet. Wayne opened with a magnificent combination of foot techniques. John responded with a flow of punches and strikes. No score yet. Both leapt in, scoring simultaneously. Then John opened with a leading punch. Wayne wheeled in, blocked the blow, and turned in with a backward roundhouse kick that arched out and towards John's head. John, eyes wide open, dropped under the kick as it passed over his head, and applied pressure on Wayne's supporting leg. Wayne allowed his momentum to spin him into a cross between a back somersault and a sideward roll. It was amazing how he recovered. No points, but the audience was roaring. A well planned exhibition could not have exceeded this spontaneous action.

As the referee restarted the contest, Wayne immediately moved forward and scored a half point with a classic stepping punch. John responded with an elbow strike, but too late. Wayne's big frame was now even more animated and alive, almost as if he were about to make a kill. John became completely calm, sidestepping the brilliant combinations thrown his way. But his eyes were alive and focused. Wayne spun in, but then changed direction with another spinning kick. John blocked both of them and pretended to do his favorite leg sweep on Wayne's left foot as it came down to the floor. Wayne anticipated and quickly raised his left knee, beginning to do a roundhouse kick, but as the foot began making its course towards the right side of John's exposed face, so John, using the driving force of his back leg, rocketed his hips forward on a collision course. With Wayne stretched out, balanced on one leg in what appeared to be a moment of suspended animation, John's left fist exploded against the skin of Wayne's throat, snapping back like a whip crack—the ultimate "killing" blow—controlled at the critical instant. It was an ideal combination of timing, focus, accuracy, strategy, and above all, courage. The referee's "*Ippon*!" was like an echo of John's spirited *kiai*, but these sounds were drowned by the great resonance of the roaring audience. We had won the contest, but more important than this, it had been a contest between true sportsmen. An *ippon* for *karate-do*.

Chapter 12

They Hit Hard, But With a Smile on Their Faces

The members of the black belt club had arranged a special dinner and cabaret for the team. Most of the cabaret, however, was supplied by some very talented members of the black belt club. The *sensei* thanked the team, the coaches, Mannie, Lisa, Nick, Jack, and all the others for their family spirit, as he put it. All had contributed, he said, to the success of the tournament.

During the evening, the *sensei* had come to Lucas and me and told us we were ready to join the morning instructor's training, that is, if we wished to do so. I could not believe it. To train with the elite squad of instructors! I remember clearly how, as young purple belts, we had nervously watched them training. The *sensei* had always impressed upon us that anyone who wished to eventually train in the Japan instructor's class should first be conditioned for at least a year or more in the morning class. In fact, this class had become somewhat famous, for a number of overseas second and third *dan* had made pilgrimages to train in it prior to going to Japan.

The first morning session was spent doing one hour of free fighting.

"For the first few days we will do a lot of *kumite*," explained the *sensei*. "In this way, you will grow to know each of the members of the class. *Jiyu kumite* is a very realistic and profound form of communication. By the end of the week, you will understand one another in a much deeper sense than you do now."

This was true, for up to now I had respected these *karateka* for what they represented. Through close interaction and confrontation, I began to know them truly for what they were, and in most cases my respect for them grew proportionately. I grew to know our *sensei* and the other *senseis* as men who gave their total spirit to each task or exercise. This came out in the *kumite*. When bowing to them, I felt their power even before we started sparring. They continually applied pressure and were forever experimenting and trying out new moves and strategies. They scored at least 10 times to my once, and my once was usually when they were trying out some new idea. Nevertheless, it motivated me like the novice golfer who comes back because of the one and only good drive he had during the game.

This week of *kumite* had, I now realized, sorted out the pecking order as something real and tangible. I knew who my seniors were in no uncertain terms, for they had laid themselves on the line. Every week the training changed. We always did a great deal of stretching—more than in the general class or black belt club. Then we would focus on certain technical or strategic areas of training.

I enjoyed Thursdays. The training was shorter, and we often gathered and communicated over tea and a light breakfast afterwards. Lucas and I, at the periphery of the table, listened as the *senseis* talked, and it was here that I discovered answers to various questions that had worried me. I heard how the *senseis* confronted their problems and how they dealt with them.

Wayne was totally open, discussing his wins and losses without any egotistical undertones. The *senseis* were equally analytical of their own techniques as well as those of others. They accepted criticism easily, always searching for a better approach to their fighting or teaching. They admired the skills of the Japanese masters. When they talked about their experiences in Tokyo's *hombu* instructor's class, everyone drew their chairs closer. It contained the highest graded experts, and its juniors were at least second or third *dans* who had achieved champion status at their particular university.

The *sensei* had left the shores of our country to train in that class numerous times. He had interacted with more than 15 generations of these experts. Each year a new generation of fighters joined the instructor's squad. They were sometimes the hardest with which to cope, for if their senior said, "Go hard on the foreigner," they would do their utmost not to let their senior down. This is, of course, the Japanese way. Apart from their superb technical skills, one also has to cope with their dedicated fighting spirit. Because of the experiences he had gone through, the *sensei* had coined a name for the Tokyo class: "The Hornet's Nest."

"Go and see for yourself," he would often say, "but first prepare well."

One morning he said, "Tournament is one thing, but that class is another matter. Those who are able to last in that class are molded into real and effective karate me. It is the ultimate test, and the ultimate training ground. Whenever I begin to feel too secure and confident of myself, I go on a pilgrimage to Japan, and my ego is quickly restored to its rightful place. There is no one top man in that class; all are top. The irony of it is that the annual All Japan Champions are not normally moved by the glory."

The *sensei* told us how, after the 1968 All Japan Championships, he had congratulated Ochi *Sensei* and told him how good he thought he was. "I no good," was Ochi's reply, "many weak points still."

"That," I thought, "is interesting and true. The moment you say, 'I am champion and best,' you are lost. Now where did I hear that?" I reflected to myself. "It doesn't matter; I just know that it is true, for the true champion cannot live in the past or rest on his laurels. The true champion is the one who is aware of the reality of the present."

The national *dan* gradings were almost upon us, and I was given the duty of taking the purple and brown belts on a *gasshuku* through the mountains. I had decided that I would give them a six-hour, nonstop *gasshuku* with only five minutes' rest every hour. It proved to be even more tiring than the previous *gasshuku* because I had to set the example and do every move with the trainees. I returned home with a tanned skin and the rare feeling of being totally cleansed.

The grading date arrived, and I felt ready to try for my second *dan*. Lucas and I had been training twice a day for the past eight weeks in both the morning and evening classes. In addition, we had also traveled to *dojos* in other areas and had sparred with their black belts. At first, our shins and forearms were bruised from the more intensive blocking and being blocked. Now I found my body had changed. It had grown hard, and I had not one bruise on me. On the other hand, I was more supple, too. It was strange that I hardly felt the effect of my opponent's blocking, no matter how hard their arms descended upon my legs. My front kick had developed mainly, I think, from training with Lucas, who had become so good at it.

I began to find that the average black belt could not stop my right front kick with only a block; I would, in most cases, break through his guard. Instead, they would have to move away, and it was through this that I also began to develop a follow-up punch to the face, that is, if my opponent moved away from my kick.

The evening before the grading, I visited friends and we enjoyed some stimulating conversation. As I walked home that mild autumn evening, I felt filled with boundless energy. I leapt up, touching the high leaves of the trees and sprinted along, dodging the telephone poles, playing cat and mouse with my shadow. A joyous feeling had entered my being, and as I slipped in between the fresh sheets of my bed, I thanked God for the gift of joy I now possessed. As sleep descended upon me, I became aware that I was smiling. I felt in harmony with the outside world of things and people that surrounded me.

Chapter 13

You Now Have to Look Deeper

The cold light of dawn was heralded by the urgent ringing of the telephone.

"I'll fetch you in 15 minutes!" It was Lucas' compelling voice.

We stopped off at a quaint coffee house for a light breakfast and chatted enthusiastically about the coming grading, going over the syllabus and discussing various tactics. It was good to have each other to lean on for moral support. I smiled inwardly, thinking of a Japanese proverb I heard somewhere, "Victims of the same disease have much to talk about." Lucas and I were quite definitely suffering from the same disease.

I had often thought and debated about the meaning of friendship. Now I didn't have to think any more. As we sat huddled together savoring the steaming aroma of the coffee in front of us, I knew I was with a friend.

Where there had been hundreds of *karateka* attempting shodan, there were now 23 of us trying for *nidan*.[*] Lucas and I knew nearly every one of the 23 examinees. We had met and interacted with them on previous *gasshukus*, championships, and courses.

We were pleased to see Neville again, and we chatted in soft voices as we warmed up on the side of the grading area.

I performed *Bassai Dai kata*. Then I had to fight two opponents, one after the other. The fighting was very different in character from tournament-style fighting. Where in tournament the contest was stopped if a point was scored, here the fighters were left to continue and only stopped if a dangerous situation developed. It was a rugged, tough kind of interaction.

---

[*] *nidan*—second *dan*

The grading ended, we lined up, bowed to the *senseis*, and left the hall. Unlike the *shodan* grading, no results were given.

A day or two later at the *dojo* I discovered that I had achieved *nidan*. Lucas, Neville, and five others had also been promoted, but the other 15 were apparently not of a high enough standard and would have to try again at the next grading in six months.

Where the *senseis* had celebrated with me on achieving first *dan*, I now noticed that hearty congratulations were certainly not the order of the day. The *sensei* came up to me and seriously said, "You have progressed, but you now have to look deeper, both at your art and at yourself. You now carry a greater responsibility." I was struck by the import not only of what he said, but how he had said it. I realized that getting a higher *dan* was not a time for flippant celebration. It was time for self-reflection. However, Jack and Lisa had passed their first *dan* gradings and had been through the initiation. It was their great moment. We celebrated with the focus upon them.

Autumn faded into winter, and the days shortened. Getting up at dawn every morning now became a willful battle. My warm bed was far more inviting than the dark, cold morning. As the weather grew colder, so the morning class became smaller, but the inner core of trainers was always there—the *sensei*, Richard, Wayne, John, Stephen, and a few other diehards.

"Where is George *Sempai*?" someone asked on morning.

"Oh, you mean 'peach blossom?'" joked the *sensei*. "When spring comes, he will be back, but when the leaves fall, he hibernates."

We found this quip funny. In fact, as we shivered and changed into cold karate gi at the break of each day, it was the spontaneous snips of humor that kept us going. I saw now why the *senseis* were such formidable men. They were constant and undaunted by weather or injury.

Chapter 14

Preparation to Enter a Foreign Arena

The winter passed, and another, and as I entered my third winter of training, an exciting development took place in my life. My employer informed me that I was soon due for a long leave. The idea that had been percolating in the back of my mind for a long time now came to fruition. Japan. But was I ready?

When I approached the *sensei* and asked him if I was ready, he answered, "Can one ever say one is totally ready?" He looked at me seriously, not revealing any signs of emotion, and continued, "You have been practicing karate for a short time—just over seven years—isn't that so?"

"Yes," I replied, not surprised by his comment. I had learned that he looked at events and things somewhat differently than the average person. Seven years to some people can be a lifetime. The *sensei*, who had been active in karate for over 20 years, saw himself as a student. "I still have much to learn," he would say if anyone flattered him.

Drawing his chair closer to mine, he leaned forward and spoke, "Seven years. It may not be a lifetime, but a life can change phenomenally in that time. You have changed. Think back to your first three years of karate. Wasn't that like embarking upon a university degree? Like doing say, a BA.? At the end of three years you qualified as a first *dan*, having acquired the basic skills or tools of your trade. Then, seeking more, you took on a further two years' study and achieved second *dan*, comparable to an honor's degree at a university, one might say.

"If you recall, that period was less rigid. You were encouraged to foster and develop your own creative talents, and you revealed these talents during the various tournaments you entered and also in the way you have been instructing the beginners. Now, for the past two years, you have extended yourself into the morning class. To me this means that you have chosen to subject yourself to extra pressures and risks. This type of challenge confronts all of those who move into the highly competitive spheres of life. In other words, it is comparable to you actively researching for your master's degree."

The *sensei* paused, shifted the position of his untouched cup of tea on the side table next to him, and I sat forward on the edge of my chair waiting for him to continue. This was the first time that he had talked in such a personal way to me.

"You have trained hard, but more important, you have immersed yourself seriously in all that this country's karate environment can offer. You have developed some uncanny strengths, but nevertheless, you still have many weaknesses. Now you are about to enter the original melting pot of *karate-do* where you will be surprised by pressures and problems you could never have imagined. There you will meet and interact with the Bjorn Borgs and Muhamad Alis of the Orient; such champions of the art as Masahiko Tanaka, Takeshi Oishi, and a select cadre of specialists. Expert fighting men, modern-day warriors with the fortitude and spirit of the *samurai* coursing through their veins."

I felt a shiver down the length of my spine. The *sensei* continued, "I have heard it said that a true *samurai* places no value on his own life. It is said, 'If a *samurai* practices introspection and self-criticism all the time and if, in addition, he is disposed to give his life where and when the need arises, he will be perfect in all the martial arts and lead an exemplary life.'

"Many of the *kenchusei** and instructors of *hombu dojo* are such men. They believe in their *do*, or way. The true martial arts, like karate, are, I believe, the modern-day vehicles of ancient *bushido.**

"You will discover when you begin to delve into the Japanese character that, although Japan was defeudalized in 1870 and was

---

* *kenchusei* — student instructors
* *bushido* — military knight's way

demilitarized by MacArthur during this century, the *bushido* spirit has not died. It still exists and is fostered in such institutions as *karate-do*."

"*Sensei*," I asked, "is *bushido* like a religion?"

"Not quite," answered the *sensei*. "The main religions of Japan are Buddhism and Shintoism. No, *bushido* grew primarily from militarism. It was a code of conduct of the *samurai*, the aristocratic warrior class that arose during the wars of the 12th century between the Taira and Minamoto clans, and came to glorious fruition in the Tokugawa period.

"Feudal lords employed *samurai* warriors who became the protectors of their community. The *samurai* were regarded as the noble class, while farmers, artisans, and businessmen belonged to the lower echelons of society. A good *samurai* dedicated himself to the cause of self-betterment, both in the physical sciences of war as well as the arts. It was his responsibility to become a living model of the *bushido* idea. Not every samurai was able to remain on the true path of *bushido*. Some of those who faltered became *ronin*, or wandering mercenaries.

"Although feudalism was abolished in the 19th century, the spirit of *bushido* exists today. It is personified in the dedication, skills, purpose, attitude, and fighting spirit of those who form the core of the economically oriented Japanese nation today.

"When a modern-day martial artist states, 'I have no castle; I make immovable mind my castle,' he is echoing one of the ideological principles of the *samurai* creed. These principles were welded to well trained physical skills and strategies, thus forging the *samurai* into a formidable opponent. However, this 'fighting machine' has a paradoxical character, for where he became an expert at destroying life, at the same time he was expected to develop all the necessary qualities for the preservation of life in its most qualitative form. Thus, humanistic aspirations and ideologies were exemplified 'in the unwritten code of laws governing the lives and conduct of the nobles of Japan...known as *bushido*.'"

I studied the *sensei's* face. It looked transformed. He was living in this communication.

"Thus, I say to you, my good friend, when you meet the Japanese, try and be sensitive to their every communication. The spirit of *bushido* still dwells within them. You will no doubt find them polite, neat, helpful, chivalrous, kind, sincere, friendly, generous, and much more, off the *dojo* floor—human beings that are hard to surpass. But when the buzzer rings and it is time to enter the training area, other virtues appear. A dramatic change takes place. The soft-spoken, Clark Kent of a man takes off his glasses and business suits, so to speak. He changes into a simple suit that transforms him into the proverbial superman. On that floor, he believes in what he is doing, dedicates himself to his art, and as a result, becomes a force with which to be reckoned."

The sensei stopped speaking, and breaking into a wide smile he said, "So, you still want to go to Japan?"

"*Osu, Sensei*! Definitely!" I responded, also smiling.

"I knew it," said he, "Your timing is good, and you have my blessing. When do you leave?"

Chapter 15

Entering the Japanese Arena

"Fasten your seatbelts," sang the clear Japanese voice of the air hostess. "We are about to land at Haneda Airport."

My sleeping legs woke up, and I straightened myself, gathering my things together. The smiling faces of my friends and family waving good-bye in the autumn afternoon seemed remote and dreamlike as the Boeing descended. We cut through a thick bank of cloud, and a string of rocky, tree-covered islands surrounded by a placid gray-green ocean was revealed. The islands, softened by an overhanging mist, stretched out like pearls. I felt nervous as we descended into this delicately shaded pastel world. The music being piped through to us by Japan Airlines had an appropriately Oriental flavor. The sound of a single instrument, the *koto* harp, its simple, clean cut yet alluring sounds drawing us into this mystical wonderland.

I was brought back to earth by the actions of the smart ground hostess who bowed to the disembarking passengers, greeting us in a polite fashion, "Welcome to Japan." She efficiently whisked us into the customs area. Within a short I had passed through customs, changed my money into *yen*, and was careening along the airport highway in a yellow taxi on my way to the Asia Center. The Asia Center was a reasonably priced residential hotel recommended by the *sensei*.

As we passed through the suburbs of Tokyo, I was enchanted by the small, neatly arranged dwellings. The scene was enlivened by innumerable quaint trees, thickly laden with pale pink flowers.

"*Sakura*," remarked the taxi driver, sensing my interest. So these were the famous Japanese cherry blossoms.

As I drank in the fragrance of the flowers, a feeling of excitement coursed through me. At the Asia Center I booked in and deposited my belongings in the tiny room that would be my home for the next three months. Within the hour, I ventured out to be devoured by the Tokyo late afternoon rush period. Assisted by pushers complete with white gloves, I was crammed into a subway car. There I stood, transfixed in the middle of this tight "sardine can," looking, no doubt, like some foreign fish—toe to toe and nose to nose with the Orient. Closer I could never get.

As we reached the Ginza station, there was no need to seek directions. Like two giant caterpillars traveling in opposite directions, the out-throng ascended the stairs while the in-throng moved down into their "sardine cans" to be shuttled off within seconds.

I surged along with the current. I had quickly learned, after having lost balance a couple of times, to reduce my stride and change to a kind of shuffling gait, which seemed to be the accepted mode of mass movement.

As our "caterpillar" emerged from the depths of the subway, it was instantly swallowed up by a sea of humanity—waves of people ebbing and flowing in all directions throughout this colorful, pulsating metropolis of shops, restaurants, bars, theaters, and street vendors. A kaleidoscope of unending sights and sounds, all underscored by a paradoxical mixture of intriguing aromas exhaled by quaint eating houses, bars, and busy cabs.

I had partaken of a hundred different sweetmeats, downed with steaming hot *sake*,* all in the company of three Japanese businessmen who had spontaneously befriended me as I entered the first restaurant. Now, having been hosted through at least 10 eating and drinking establishments, I marched down the main Ginza thoroughfare, arm in arm with these incredible strangers, singing a Japanese song.

They delivered me to the front door of the Asia Center. I had been treated like a king, and by total strangers. They had not allowed me to put my hand in my pocket.

---

* *sake*—rice wine

As my head touched the pillow, I fell into a deep sleep, waking up a day and a half later. It was Monday morning and time to visit the *hombu dojo*.

Modern Japan, with its busy streets, cars, and people, dissolved behind me as I stepped into the side entrance of the JKA *hombu dojo*. I ascended the stairs, and my senses were alerted by a set of sounds that grew louder as I approached the first floor landing. I felt like a moth being drawn towards the flame. These were familiar sounds. Sounds of feet moving across a wooden floor, *kiais*, the sharp orders and count of a *sensei*, but there was something compellingly different from what I had ever heard back home. What I now heard sent a cold shiver up my spine. It was different; that was all I knew. The very building seemed to vibrate in sympathy to whatever was taking place up there.

I stopped in front of a fragile, wooden sliding door with a frosted glass panel. Before I could knock, the door was opened by a small beaming man who bowed and welcomed me, taking my shoes and putting them in a rack, which was full with an assortment of shoes and sandals.

"My name is Seto," he said. "We have been expecting you. How is your *sensei*?"

"Very well," I replied, surprised at the good English Mr. Seto spoke. He led me into a small office. At the far end was a big desk, behind which sat a very important-looking Japanese gentleman.

"Mr. Takagi, Director of the JKA," announced Mr. Seto. "I will translate for you." This didn't seem necessary, for Mr. Takagi, a stocky man in his late fifties, leaned forward across his desk, looking at me as if studying my every feature. I was startled by his short-clipped sentences, which were free of any frills.

"For what purpose you visit Japan?"

"To study karate," I responded.

"Why you do karate?" he shot at me. I turned to Seto for moral support, but his sweet smile grew into a wide, happy grin. The question was so simple, I reflected. I could not think of a clever answer, so I simply said, "Because I love karate."

Mr. Takagi sat back, nodded his head a few times, a serious expression on his face, and unexpectedly broke into a spontaneous smile that became an infectious chuckle. We were all laughing as he proceeded to pour tea for us. As I raised the cup and sipped the steaming, light green liquid, I could not prevent my hand from trembling. The training seemed to be reaching a peak, judging by the crescendo of sounds that penetrated the thin office walls. Mr. Takagi was quite unconcerned by this noise. He asked what was to me an unlikely question, especially considering the unbearable tension that had built up inside me.

"What you think of Japanese green tea?" he asked. I hadn't really thought about how it tasted.

"Uh...very good," I ventured, at which he proceeded to top up my cup. It occurred to me then that this tea tasted more bitter than anything I had ever consumed in my life.

Judging by the sudden quietness, I concluded that the training had ended. It was one o'clock in the afternoon.

"You wish to take practice?" he questioned.

"Yes, please, Mr. Takagi," I nervously replied. Out of the corner of my eye I noticed that a karate man had entered the room. He searched through some files, found what he wanted, bowed again, and made his exit. Judging by his moist brow and damp *karate gi*, he had, no doubt, been part of that class. I was fascinated by his serene attitude but more so by the fact that he was the tallest Japanese I had yet seen. Sensing my interest, Mr. Takagi offered, "He berry big Japanese. Mista Tabata, berry strong instructor, but he such good manner!" Mr. Takagi's pronunciation of the word "very" intrigued me.

"Mr. Takagi, which training class should I attend?" I asked.

"Of course, instructor training!" he said, as if it went without saying. "You now old *nidan*...neh?"

"Can I start tomorrow?" I asked, nervously.

"Good idea!" he exclaimed, rising to meet a group of men who had entered the office. Seto led me out and treated me to a delicious *sukiyaki*, a steak and vegetable meal, informing me that I was to report to the *dojo* for training at 11:30 the following morning.

Chapter 16

The Hornet's Nest — Japan Squad Training

I arrived at the *dojo* early and entered the training hall where a general class was in progress. At the far end of the expansive, shiny wooden floor was a small wooden shrine. To the left was the only splash of color, a large, white Japanese flag with a red rising sun dominating its center. To the right of the shrine was a board with five guiding principles inscribed on it: "Strive for perfection of character. Be faithful. Endeavor. Respect others. Refrain from violent behavior." These were both in Japanese and in English characters. Along one wall was a row of *makiwaras*. The only other pieces of equipment were a huge sandbag, which was suspended in the rear right-hand corner of the *dojo*, and a large mirror on the opposite wall.

I noticed there were a number of Westerners in the class, no doubt people living and working in Japan. One instructor, assisted by two younger sub-instructors, conducted the class. The training was very similar to our general class back home. It ended at 11:30, and the students sat upright forming two straight lines facing the shrine wall. They meditated for about two minutes and repeated after the instructor the five maxims in Japanese:

> *Jinkaku kansei ni tsutomuru koto.*
> *Makoto no michi o mamoru koto.*
> *Doryoku no seshin o yashinau koto.*
> *Reigi o omonzuru koto.*
> *Kekki no you o imashimuru koto.*

These words were repeated with a spirit of fortitude that left the atmosphere charged and electrified even after the students had moved off to change or to practice on the side. I bowed, stepped onto the floor, and began lightly striking a *makiwara*. It had an un-usual feel to it—just enough give. I preferred this sheaved straw to the rubber pads to which I was accustomed.

A number of young, clean-cut looking black belts filed onto the back corner of the floor near to me. Some sat, conversing quietly, each going smoothly and easily through his own stretching routine. Some of them were doing light free sparring. Not sure of what I should be doing, I kept my gaze towards the *makiwara*, but I was able to observe their actions out of the corner of my eye. What I saw amazed me. This was the most flexible group I had ever seen. Total splits in all directions seemed to be a natural habit to them. Then a stock Westerner with a crew cut arrived and walked straight up to me. "*Osu*! My name's Gary," he said, bowing to me. I intro-duced myself, asking him to guide me with regard to the *dojo* pro-tocol.

"Sure," he said, "come and stretch with me." His voice had a marked American drawl. Gary was more my match, both of us be-ing far less flexible than the student instructors , or *kenchusei*, as Gary described them.

"The *kenchusei* usually stretch for about 30 minutes before the class," he said, gradually coaxing my legs out as wide as they would go, using his own feet as levers and holding onto my belt with his hands.

"Why so long?" I asked. "They don't seem to need it."

"Because their seniors have told them to do so," he explained, pushing my legs to their aching limit. "Breathe more deeply and try to relax your face and neck," he encouraged. "In just a moment, the 'big guns' will arrive, so be ready and do just what I do." We changed positions, and I stretched his legs.

"Oh, man," whispered Gary suddenly, looking across at the *kenchusei* group. "Guess who has arrived?"

"Who?" I asked.

"The animal," he said slowly, only loud enough for me to hear. I stole a quick look, and what I saw caused a violent reaction within my innards. A square, blunt-faced, powerhouse stepped onto the floor. His narrow eyes were set deeply into a clean-shaven head.

He ignored the group, moved past them, and headed for the sand-bag with deliberate mechanical strides. He was different from the other athletes. What now had entered the floor looked less like a human being and more like a gigantic bull terrier. It is strange how one can move placidly through life and then unexpectedly come across a total stranger who instantly spells danger. My entire being had just told me that this man was "trouble."

With my heart beating somewhat harder and faster against my ribcage, I swallowed the invisible lump in my throat and asked Gary, "Is he an instructor?"

"No, he is also a *kenchusei*...been second *dan* for about two years now...a real loner...the other day he put his only friend in the hospi-tal.

"But I thought we were supposed to control..."

"Control in this class is a relative thing. What may appear to be a very hard blow to the average person from the general class is a controlled blow to this group. But yes, Mr. Sado* often goes too far."

"Don't the seniors stop him?"

"Yes, but then it is often too late. He goes through the ritual of kneeling and bowing his head in penance. Their theory is to for-give the culprit if he shows enough repentance. This is in the hope that he will mend his ways, but so far this leopard hasn't changed his spots. I guess he needs a good lesson from someone. But who's to do it?"

"Search me," I said, feeling as timid as a lamb.

The "big guns" stepped onto the floor. The *kenchusei*, then Gary and I sprang upright and bowed to the impressive group of instruc-tors (fourth *dan* and above) who filed onto the floor and formed the straightest line I had ever seen. We, the *kenchusei*, lined up beside them, with me as the junior on the far end of the line. A distant clock struck 12:00. Nakayama *Sensei* kneeled in front of us. We bowed, and the training began.

---

* Mr. Sado—a fictional name

A command had us all in a large circle doing warm-up calisthenics conducted by one of the *kenchusei*, who led us through example with a short-clipped utterance every time there was a change in exercise. This brisk limbering lasted only about five minutes, as it was expected that we had warmed up before the class.

Next, still in a circle, we did repetition punching rooted in a front stance. Each member of the class counted to 10, starting with the most senior and working around the circle to me. The actions were dynamic, and we had completed 100 kicks on each side before the master ordered, "Yame!"

I felt more exhausted from this opening 15 minutes than I had ever felt in my own country. After the first 50 kicks, my legs had become like lead weights. One or two of the trainees had missed the odd repetitions, but Sado, I noticed, had applied himself totally to every move.

During the 30 seconds of rest, it dawned on me that my abnormal exhaustion stemmed from a sense of insecurity and over-tension. This alien environment, the demanding standard of excellence, the strange language, fast pace, and to cap it all, "the animal," all contributed to my present feeling.

For the next 30 minutes we practiced a series of interactions with a partner. Before each action, the master carefully demonstrated and described the technicalities. His demonstrations were intricately clear, but my sparse understanding of Japanese didn't allow me to comprehend any deeper meaning that, no doubt, he was communicating verbally.

We were half way through this special *kumite* when both my forearms began to ache badly. The only thing that relieved me was that Sado was in the same row as me. Thus, in changing from partner to partner, I had not yet had to face him. However, this was but a small compensation, where I had been on the receiving end of the most potent front kick I had ever faced. The attacking side was required to do front kicks on us with the expressed purpose of making contact with our stomachs using direct force, strategy, or both. Over the 15 minutes of repetitive blocking, we practiced three different approaches.

In the first, *go no sen*, we had to try to move directly backwards, blocking the kick, and then return forwards doing a counter. My main problem was that I could never seem to propel myself far away enough from my opponent's foot, and thus I was unable to ride the force. I took most of it on the forearm and sometimes on the stomach. These short men had the uncanny knack of suddenly developing the longest legs.

In the second approach, *tai sabaki*, we were required to pivot to the side, blocking the kick and almost simultaneously delivering the counter measure. This was comparable to the sidestep of a bullfighter. Here I found I was not dropping and rotating my hips quickly enough, and two or three times I took too much impact and struggled quickly to get air back into my lungs without revealing the fact to my attacker.

With the third approach, *sen no sen*, we had to take the initiative earlier and move directly forwards into the attack just as the kick started, countering at the same time. This approach is also sometimes knows as *kamikaze* or suicide approach. I found that when I luckily moved in early enough it worked, and I did not hurt myself. Mostly, I sensed the attack too late. My late forward propulsion caused my blocking arm to clash with a fast-moving shin bone. The very bones of my forearms felt bruised as we made the last change, and the big instructor, Tabata, stood facing me. I expected the worst, but it turned out to be one of the best confrontations for me. He was very kind, slowing his attack down and giving me helpful advice, not via the spoken word, bur rather through a very comprehensible sign language.

For the next 15 minutes we were the attackers, and my shin bones became the painful victims of repetitive blocking. For the last 15 minutes of the class, we practiced *kata*, and the prolonged intensity of the training brought a red flush to my face and a burning to the soles of my feet. I had never felt like this before.

I literally dragged myself out of the *dojo* like a wet rag. I was too tired to eat. Back at my room I swallowed volumes of liquid — anything on which I could lay my hands. I then fell on my bed and rested.

On waking the next day, I felt stiff and sore all over, and to make things worse, I found myself limping towards the communal bathroom. I had two huge blisters on the soles of my feet. My arms from wrist to elbow were swollen and all colors of the rainbow. Desperately, I telephoned Seto, telling him what I felt and looked like.

"Ah!" he said, "Jet lag. Your body not yet ready. But you start training, so you never stop. Go to drugstore and tape yourself. Be like *samurai*. Never give up."

I did what he said and attended the second day of training and the third. By the fifth day, I felt nauseous. The training had been similar to the other days except for one difference: We did different attacks on each consecutive day. By this time, I was so covered in tap, I must have looked like a mummy. In addition to my discolored arms and legs and raw feet, I now had a number of extra swollen features—my small finger from blocking with an open hand; my right big toe from accidentally kicking someone's bent elbow instead of his stomach; and a swollen nose from stupidly going forwards into my attacker's punch with my eyes closed. All of this, and I had not yet faced Sado.

As we finished on Friday, Seto told me that there was no more instructor's training until Monday. "You take good rest, see sites of Tokyo." The first step in my recuperation program set up by Seto was a visit to an immaculate bathhouse where the healing elements of hot and cold water, massage, tranquillity, and friendship were administered.

I awoke on Monday morning to the sound of rain droplets against my bedroom window. My mind felt light and refreshed, as if a thick bank of cloud had been removed. My body had not yet healed completely, but it was well on its way, and I hummed a little tune as I showered, making ready to leave for the *dojo*.

Chapter 17

The Master Speaks—Your Whole Body is an Eye

Where we had concentrated upon techniques and tactics in the past week, this week consisted mainly of confrontations that put or reflexes, timing, and ability to respond on the firing line.

The master had cleverly conceived an approach of gradually stepping up the degree of difficulty of the confrontations. On the first day, the defenders had to stand in a fixed position. The attacker could stand as close as he liked and deliver single blows that had to be deflected without blinking an eye. The attacker announced what blow he would be delivering, but he could do it from any distance he chose and use any timing. In other words, wait and suddenly strike, not necessarily at a regular tempo.

On the second day, we had to do the same thing, but this time the attacker could do any of two announced attacks. For example, he would announce *jodan* or *chudan* and proceed to do either of the two.

On the third day we weren't restricted to a fixed position, and were thus allowed movement, except that the attacker could move in with any one attack without warning. I found that I had to resort mainly to *go no sen*, that is, moving away as the attack came. I wasn't confident enough to move in with *sen no sen*.

Oishi *Sensei*, seven times All Japan champion, amazed me. His timing and responsing were uncanny. No matter what attack I launched, be it punch, kick, or strike, he moved forwards scoring on me before I could finish it. It was almost as if he were reading my mind. His control was superb, and I was never hurt by him. Interacting with masters like him and Tabata had restored some of my confidence.

But the fourth day proved to be "black Thursday" for me. Before the class, I was stretching and watching some of the *kenchusei* doing light sparring. I felt a tap on my shoulder.

"*Sukoshi kumite* (a little free fighting)," uttered the gruff voice of Sado. Facing him was as bad as I had imagined it might be. He stood, hands at his sides, I assumed the regular fighting stance and tried to look in his face. He looked not at me but through me as if I didn't exist. Then, hands still at his sides, he proceeded to walk at me. It was if some invisible force emanated from him, causing me to move backwards. For the next minute or two he walked while I backpedaled, traversing the length and breadth of the large *dojo*. Not one blow had been struck when the buzzer rang for the start of the class, but this animal of a man had controlled me in a manner that I did not like at all.

As we meditated, I remembered the words of my *sensei*, "They will seek *kyo* in you and attack *kyo*. And the attack will be directed at where your greatest weakness lies. It may exist in any one of these realms—your body, your mind, or your spirit."

Sado, I now realized, had managed to capture my spirit.

During the warm-up I spoke to myself, rationalizing that he was only flesh and blood like me and that I had only two alternatives: To stand up to him or to be completely trodden under foot. Through all of the conditioning training, my mind was not totally present in my body. I did the movements easily and automatically. My mind had leapt ahead to the *kumite* training that I knew was inevitable. I also knew that I would face Sado again, before the day ended.

Sado became my invisible opposition, the theoretical victim of every technique that I launched into that circle of energy and fire.

The master broke the circle and told us to form a line, a queue facing the most senior members of the class. This was it, I thought. Today's interaction had progressed to a stage where the defender faced a line of attackers. Taking his turn, each member of the line could deliver any one technique at the defender without telling him what it was to be. After every one of us had delivered one attack, the next in seniority would become the defender. I would be on last and did not savor the idea.

It was well past one o'clock when Sado faced the line as defender. From the back, I watched him facing up to the various seniors. For the first time, I noticed that Mr. Takagi was watching the training from a doorway situated behind Sado. What I had observed was that Sado was very aggressive, tended to be wild, often tried too hard, and sometimes lost his balance. From his posture, I decided that he was open to a left front kick. I planned to approach him timidly, suddenly create spirit by kiaiing loudly, pause, and a split second later deliver my front kick.

It worked. The kick sailed through, and he almost fell over his feet rushing to counter me. But before he could get at me, the master told the next defender to take Sado's place. Almost everybody had been on, and it would soon be my turn to face the line. It came, and all I saw was Sado at the back end of the fast-shortening queue. Then he was on me. He gave a bloodcurdling yell and stormed forwards, unleashing a running combination of kicks and punches. This eruption sent me reeling backwards, careening back into the fragile windows that framed the doorway. We both landed in the office amid a shower of shattered glass and wood.

I felt embarrassed as we were hoisted out of the mess and led back to the floor with two of the seniors admonishing my adversary for breaking the "on-blow attack" rule.

This was not the end of my relationship with Sado, I thought. This was but the beginning. I had found myself a rival...or had he found me?

The following Wednesday proved to be another one of those black days. The training had been going well. I felt energetic, and my body was in fine condition. Although the blocking was still intense, I was no longer bruising. I had also learned to deflect the kicks more successfully, but we were onto line work again. This time the degree of difficulty for the defender was greater. He started with his back to the wall, and the attackers could do any one attack on him. This put tremendous stress upon the defender, as he was unable to escape backwards. There were two alternatives—*sabaki*, pivoting sideways; or *sen no sen*, moving into the attack.

I noticed that the pressure seemed to be too great, even for the highest *dans*. One All Japan champion had been successfully moving in on each attack, when at last he faced Tabata, who used the tactic of waiting. I remember how Stephen had rattled me with this approach many years ago. The trainee made a number of false starts, which no doubt took the edge off his timing. When Tabata's front kick came, he moved in just a fraction too late, taking half of the impact on his forearm and other half on his abdomen. He doubled up, the wind knocked out of him. In an instant, a senior instructor, Mabuchi, attended to him, applying a resuscitation technique that revived the trainee within seconds.

My turn came. I felt ready and full of spirit as I faced the first attacker. This feeling was short-lived. Mori artfully hooked my front foot away with his front foot, and I went sailing to the floor. I was shaken. The next attacker spun around, and I pivoted to the side, but not quickly enough. His back fist strike made contact with my hand, causing me to slap my own cheek. It was smarting as I faced number three, Oishi. Before I could think, he closed the distance like a gale. All I felt was a light tap on the chin. If there was ever any time in my life when my head could have been taken off my shoulders, it was then. Yet Oishi had acted with benevolence, a true sportsman. But what of Sado and some of the other unknowns? Could I rely on them? No, I couldn't afford to take that chance. A fear gripped me, and at that moment I resorted to prayer. Inwardly I asked, "God, help me. Please help me face up to these men. What must I do? Give me what I need." Strangely, at that point, the master called a halt and spoke to me.

"You...too much thinking...you look only with two eyes...don't forget your whole body is an eye."

I did not quite understand, but his few words had given me spirit. As I was about to start with the next opponent, he added, "Hips more tight. Make body one unit."

I managed to block the next few attackers but could not get my counter technique in. Then Sado faced me, his arms hanging loosely at his sides. He walked towards me as he had done on Thursday. With the wall behind me, I could not back away, so I rooted myself firmly, setting my gaze on the triangle formed by his shoulders and nose. I tried to see him generally, rather than looking specifically at any one part of him. When Sado was very close to me, he stopped and tried to outstare me. I didn't allow myself to be taken in by the stare. I concentrated on seeing all of him. My legs began vibrating from the tension of my bent knees, but my poise didn't waver. He tried to distract me by bringing his hands together with a loud clapping noise and followed up immediately with an unorthodox bola punch to my head. I blocked, but a second, unexpected punch glanced off the side of my head. As a third was on its way, I blocked it and caught his wrists with my hands. He reacted by bringing the crown of his head down in the direction of my nose. I avoided the direct impact and took the head butt against my chest. Without realizing it, my right elbow homed in against his cheekbone. For a brief moment, he looked dumb struck, almost as if saying, "Who are you to be hitting me?" Then, like a hungry hyena, he screamed and sank his teeth into my forearm, biting hard to free himself. We broke apart and, like two incensed fighting cocks, flew at each other again, but the instructors intervened, pulling us apart. One of them took him aside and reprimanded him in no uncertain terms. He hung his head, saying only, "*Osu, osu, osu,*" all the time. For the next few weeks, Sado and I didn't confront each other again. The instructors were without doubt seeing to it that we remained apart.

Chapter 18

Human Beings Emerge

As I passed the office on my way home, Tabata *Sensei* called me, saying, "Tomorrow you please come to my *sayonara* party. Also welcome party for Mista Tanaka. All instructors come."

Evidently, Tabata *Sensei* was about to depart for some country where he would be instructing. Tanaka, the world champion who had visited my country and who had impressed me so much, was returning from abroad. The instructors arranged a party to honor both of them. I bowed deeply a number of times, thanking Tabata for the honor of being invited. He left, saying, "You good fighting spirit."

He had made my day. With a spring in my step, I walked to the subway station singing a Japanese ditty about a telephone conversation sung to the tune of "London Bridge is Falling Down."

> *"Moshi moshi*
> *Ano-ne, ano-ne,ano-ne,*
> *Moshi moshi ano-ne, ah-so, desu ka."*

The passing people smiled.

* * *

The restaurant was a simple construction of wood and *tatami** with separate areas for various groups of people divided by a lattice of cleanly washed wood. At the head of each area was an alcove with a simple, yet exquisite, flower arrangement. A long, low, shiny wooden table graced the center of each area. The instructors

---

* *tatami* — straw mats

seated themselves on the floor and Isaka, the toastmaster for the evening, showed Gary and me where to sit.

We waited quietly until a tray of Kirin beer arrived. Three of the *kenchusei* sprang up and poured drinks for the seniors, who held their glasses. When all the glasses were filled, Isaka made a short speech honoring Tabata and Tanaka, who were seated in the front of the alcove. Then, to a rousing *kampai*,* we downed the beer in one gulp. I was pleased that it was very light beer and that the glasses were small. Then other kenchusei moved around the table, bowing to each recipient and refilling his glass.

"This pouring of drinks is an important social custom," pointed out Gary. "It is etiquette to do so graciously, at the right time. Come on, grab a bottle and do your round."

I moved around on my knees, unable to disguise my clumsiness. The instructors were dignified, yet warm. Most thanked me in Japanese, while only one or two spoke in English.

Tanaka said, "Your country very beautiful." I replied, saying that Japan was wonderful. The atmosphere gradually loosened as the first course of food arrived.

The instructors began to intersperse and move away from their initial, formalized positions to sit and converse with the various sub-groups, which changed all the time. The beer pouring tradition was a clever method of causing ongoing interaction. I noticed that although beer was used at the start, certain instructors moved on to a variety of drinks, some to *sake*, others to Coke or juice, and others to whiskey. There was a marked change in these people as their formal masks began to drop, revealing humorous and friendly human beings.

I could not believe it when even Sado came across and poured me a drink. I reciprocated later and thought I caught the faint trace of a smile on his lips. But I wasn't sure.

The spirit of the party grew with each new sweetmeat that was placed upon the table. At one point the whole group sang a

---

* *kampai*—a toast, "Cheers!"

samurai song and then each member of the party did a solo while the rest clapped out a steady rhythm. When it was my turn, I sang the national anthem of my country, which was very well received. It seemed to break the ice, for I had hardly sat down again when Oishi, Seto, and a group of kenchusei called us to join them. Oishi pulled out a sheet of paper, announcing that one of the *kenchusei* had drawn a picture, which he presented to me.

I joined their rollicking laughter when I saw what it was—a cartoon drawing of two gawky individuals in *karate gi* with one biting the other's finger. It was all in such good spirit, I wondered if they had shown it to Sado.

Suddenly, Isaka stood up, said something in Japanese, and everybody took their original places and sat in a formal kneeling position. A short speech was made followed by bows and exclamations from various instructors. Then Isaka closed the event in typical, clean-cut *samurai* fashion.

As I was putting on my shoes in the foyer, Oishi and Seto called me aside. Oishi said, "You must soon take *sandan* (third degree black belt) examination." I looked disbelievingly at him. They glanced at each other and Seto added, "Nakayama *Shihan*,[*] he speak to us, okay you take *sandan* next month."

I really didn't know what to say. "*Osu!*" I replied, looking at them for a lead.

"But now you take very hard training, okay?" Oishi looked me straight in the eyes.

"Osu, *Sensei!*" I answered. "*Domo arigato gozai masu.*"[*]

Gary and I shared a taxi. It didn't take us long to realize that we had both been invited to enter the third *dan* gradings.

"How many times have you tried for third *dan*?" Gary asked me.

"First time," I replied.

"You don't stand much chance," he said. "I've tried three times. This is my fourth attempt."

---

[*] *shihan*—master
[*] *domo arigato gozai masu*—thank you very much

"What!" I said, aghast. "Why is that?"

"Because this is a very severe test. They take this *dan* level very seriously. It is what they call the 'fighting *dan*.' It is a big breakthrough, like passing from amateur to professional level."

"What does one have to do?" I questioned.

"Very simple. Do your favorite *kata* and then fight five men in a row." He boxed me lightly on my shoulder and grinned. "It's tough, my friend, really tough. I know."

"Whom do you have to fight?" I asked.

"Two new second *dans*, two from your own group of examinees, and one instructor ranked fifth *dan* or above. And you fight him last, when the others have already thrown everything at you."

"Wow!" I responded. "It must take a lot of stamina to get through that."

"Not only that. There is something else..."

"What?" I demanded.

"Control often seems to go out of the window. The guys get over-excited, and it can become dangerous. You have to be careful that you don't also become so excited that you fail to see what is going on. I made that mistake and ended up with a broken nose." Gary paused. His face was deadly serious. "All I can say is keep calm in the face of the storm. My advice to you is to fight strongly and fairly, but if someone happens to lose his self-control and makes contact unfairly, then hit him back immediately: an eye for an eye. This I found to be the soundest method of restoring order."

As I walked down the long, narrow, bamboo-lined driveway towards the Asia Center, I knew I was savoring the bittersweet of life. The coveted prize was within my grasp, but at what price?

Chapter 19

Creativity Becomes a Desperate Need

The training became geared towards the international dan gradings. Our workload and volume was gradually increased until we were doing double the amount of training, double the amount of repetitions, double the amount of techniques. As we were reaching the peak of this marathon type training, I felt a deep tiredness creeping up on me.

One day in the circle, we had repeated 1,000 punches and were starting the second 1,000 when the master approached a *kenchusei* training next to me. I heard him shouting at the man. He happened to be in a very low stance.

"More down...more lower!" The *kenchusei* replied with "*Osu!*" and looked as if he would disappear through the floor if he went any lower. The master kept doing this, and then it dawned on me that he was using English, speaking to a Japanese! He had never done this before. But he persisted, "Why you not hear? Down, I say!"

The penny dropped. I was in a high stance. It cold only be me with whom he was communicating, so I dropped into a low stance. Immediately, the master left the tired *kenchusei* and moved away to another part of the class. The Japanese sometimes have a strange way of communicating. The master's indirect approach had a profound effect on me later. I thought to myself that without embarrassing me, he had communicated something of value, for I had eventually responded to his message, and communication was satisfactorily completed. We had spoken to each other, in a sense, a profound sense. I had much to learn from these people. What if I had not sensed his communication? If I nearly missed his point, then how many previous communications had I missed due to my insensitivity? For the first time, I realized that being sensitive and open to the communication of others was a very important asset, especially when considering the process of survival. For the first time, I knew that every utterance, every move, and every non-move was a form of communication. In order to cope with them I must learn to read and interpret their actions. They spoke with their bodies, not a language of empty words, but a language of doing, filled with thrust, energy, and emotions, of truth, explicit to the moment at hand. When pitting myself against martial artists, their wisdom would rub off on me, a touchstone to clarity. Interacting with them demanded clarity. I thought about my heritage and what I had read, "A wise man is mightier than a strong man."

It was impossible for foolishness to last long on the *hombu dojo* floor. It had to be replaced by wisdom, for only a wise man could survive the human chess game taking place in that arena.

A strange thought crossed my mind. Here I was in the middle of an alien culture and now, for the first time, I was experiencing the value and truth of my own religious background. A verse from Proverbs gave purpose to my quest: "Iron sharpens iron, and one man sharpens another."

With the *dan* gradings near at hand, I noticed that the volume of work was gradually decreasing, while the intensity was on the increase. In other words, we were changing from long, repetitive workouts to shorter, explosive training. Where before the accent had been on endurance and on a great volume of formalized training, now it allowed each of us to express our own creativity.

Where previously we had been restricted, now there was freedom to test and express our own tactics, speed, rhythm, distancing, and timing. The pace had more than trebled. We were now "sprinting" in short bursts, so to speak, rather than "jogging." The confrontations were short, and the actions like lightning.

I was very surprised when Tanaka *Sensei* invited me to free fight with him every day. Our first confrontation was 20 minutes of free fighting. Where "the animal" had disturbed me with his rough, aggressive tactics, Tanaka's approach caused me to become at first relaxed, then bewildered, and finally frightened. He would lag forwards, moving softly like a relaxed panther. His face was calm, communicating not the slightest hint of any aggression except for two smoldering coals of fire, his eyes. They had a hypnotic effect and were all the more penetrating, since they were framed within a clean-cut thatch of short, spiky, black hair. Within the first minute of kumite with him, I knew I was facing an expert of experts—not a predatory powerhouse like Sado, but a deadly specialist who did not waste an ounce of energy.

The fight opened with me, relaxed, moving to and fro. Tanaka had created a rhythm. He would move towards me and then a little away. He kept doing this. I watched him intently. The third time, he came close and dropped his guard. I dropped and threw a reverse punch at his open chest. He deftly swiveled to the side. I missed him and began standing up-. Catching my arm with one of his hands, he leapt into the air, entwining his legs around my unsteady hips and with sudden explosive force, he wrenched me downwards, flattening my back against the floor He had used a flying scissors technique. Still trapped like a fly in a spider's web, I felt the sharp slap of a well controlled heel to my chest. Like magic, he entwined himself and was gliding again, telling me to rise. My previous relaxed feeling had now turned into bewilderment and fear.

As we sparred on, I felt more and more powerless. Everything I tried, he turned to his advantage. My best attack, the front kick, had no effect on him. As I raised my knee to kick, his hands easily caught my leg, and every time this happened, he threw me in different ways using a variety of unique and surprising counters. His counter always found my most vulnerable area, and his controlled blow was like a firm, stinging slap. Once, thinking he had lost concentration, I tried to do a left roundhouse kick to his head. My leg was only halfway on course when his left leg lashed the skin of my stomach.

It was as if his techniques were over before they started. One saw nothing coming, and he was suddenly calm again, but not those eyes.

I felt like a wretched mouse being toyed with by a well-fed cat who had no interest in eating me, just yet.

I went home in pain. It was not a deep-seated muscular soreness, and there was no bone pain, but there was a soreness that was much more revealing—my skin was red and on fire.

Every time he worked with me it was the same. I did not seem to be improving, and I began to dread our daily confrontations. At last, I began having sleepless nights, and if I did get to sleep at all, I kept having a recurring nightmare. There was a dark, black cloud that appeared and always began to envelop me. I would strike out wildly, but felt it smothering me. Always I became weaker and weaker, my limbs moving as if in slow motion.

There were just three days to go before the gradings. I was working against Oishi. We had been chasing each other across the length of the *dojo* floor, doing our favorite combinations on each other—moving target work.

I would try my combinations on him. He backpedaled like a mongoose moving away from a cobra. It was very hard to reach him. I only managed it once or twice. But he was phenomenal. He covered such a great distance in a short time. He would face me and always say first, "You ready?" Then, try as I may, his explosive hips and giant strides tore at me like a Sidewinder missile finding its target. Then we would rest for a few seconds, and it would start all over again, my turn to chase him.

The humid summer days and the intense effort caused me to run rivers of perspiration. Once, Oishi and I both slipped and fell in the sweat. I thought he would kill me, but he lay on the floor laughing, finally saying, "You very clever fighter...make deep river...me nearly drown." I found that very funny.

Chapter 20

Learning the Art of Asking the Right Questions

As the class ended, Tanaka approached me. "Oh, my goodness," I thought, "not again!" As if reading my mind, he said, "No *kumite* today. I ask question. You have free time now?"

"*Osu, Sensei*," I replied, bowing and nodding in the affirmative.

"Okay, you change, we take lunch together."

As I showered and changed, the weirdest notions passed through my mind. On the one hand, I was excited and pleased about lunch but, on the other hand, words repeated themselves in my mind: "So the big cat is hungry. What is he going to eat? Hope it's not me."

We lunched at a western-style MacDonald's restaurant. Contrary to my expectations, I found him very amiable and easy to talk to.

"You like karate?" he asked.

"Very much, *Sensei*," I replied, "but I don't feel I am very good at the moment."

"Why?" he questioned, raising his eyebrows and tilting his head to the side. I could still not reconcile myself to the fact that this was the same man who had been the major cause of my nightmares.

"Well, *Sensei*..." I picked my words carefully. "I feel so unconfident when I fight you. I feel as if I am a new beginner."

"How long you study karate?" he asked.

"Nearly eight years," I replied.

"Oh, I study karate nearly 20 years," he said. "Karate road very long. Sometimes up, sometimes down. I also have same feeling before but, please, you never give up." His expression grew serious. "I think soon big change happen in you."

"*Sensei*," I asked, "please, will you tell me what my biggest problem is?"

"You!" he said, grinning broadly. He had taken me by surprise again. I laughed nervously, and he added, "Of course, everybody have same problem." He went on, "Your technique and spirit very good, but you need more understanding of distancing."

"What do you mean, *Sensei*?" I queried.

"I not speak...you must study, then soon discover for yourself..." His change of position told me that this subject was now closed. We ate and talked about my family, his family, Japanese customs, and about my country. As coffee was being poured, I asked him how he had trained before winning the world championship.

"Much general training as we do now," he told me. "The few weeks before championship I sometimes sleep in *dojo*, and do own special training." Tanaka looked very relaxed. He had folded his legs neatly, and now sat perched upon his chair in a cross-legged position. If I had tried that, I would have fallen off the chair.

He went on. "Sometimes I sit late at night on *dojo* floor, alone, and write on piece of paper, 'WHAT IS CHAMPION?' Many times I write, 'WHAT IS CHAMPION?' One evening all *dojo* floor covered with 'WHAT IS CHAMPION?' and so I ask question and wait, then train. Then one day I receive answer to what is champion."

"When was that, *Sensei*?" I asked.

"Of course, the day I win the championship!" he smiled. I smiled too, sheepishly, feeling so foolish for not realizing. No doubt, this Tanaka was always a step or two ahead.

As I clung to the leather hang strap maintaining my balance in the speeding subway coach, Tanaka's spirit was still with me. His way of thinking fascinated me. Keeping time to the staccato rapping of the speeding train wheels, a voice inside me kept repeating, "What is distancing?"

From the moment the Thursday class began, the atmosphere was intense. Without allowing us to warm up, the master announced, "*Jiyu kumite. Hajime*!" Every five minutes, we changed partners, and this went on for the full hour.

I fought everybody in the class except Tanaka and Sado. The other instructors were "switched on," and I felt that all their fury was unleashed upon me. I gained the impression that they were working lightly with each other, but when they faced me it was as if they were bulls and I a red flag.

I tried to use my greater size to hold them off or to intimidate them, but gradually they wore me down until I began moving in a mindless sea of action, sweat, and tiredness. I was no longer capable of thinking or anticipating. I released blows, took blows, fell down, stood up, kept going. I no longer worried about being injured. Some inner spirit drove me on. Winning or losing became non-existent. All that mattered was to keep going. It was as if someone else was doing the fighting. When the master ordered, "*Yame!*" it was as though I was awakened from a dream. Then we meditated. I existed in a timeless zone, disappeared, merging with the surroundings, emptied of all worldly thoughts. Nothing mattered.

The class ended, and I realized that we had been sitting for over half an hour, yet had felt like a few minutes.

The master summoned me and told me to take Friday off and relax because I was grading on Saturday. As I bowed to him and started making my way out of the *dojo*, he called me back and said, "A truly big man must first learn to become a small man." With that, he closed the communication by calling another *karateka* to him.

I walked slowly along the street, a new line added to my self-made koan:* "What is distancing; what is small man?"

It was only after I reached the Asia Center that I realized I had covered the seven-mile distance on foot instead of taking the usual subway ride. Soaking in a hot bath, it occurred to me that I had today closed the seven-mile distance between *hombu dojo* and Asia Center unconsciously. "What is distancing?" I sang out aloud. Then, surveying my big frame filling the tiny tub, I wondered how on earth I could become a small man. What did the master mean? As I rubbed my body down with a towel, I thought, "Maybe he

---

* *koan*—a riddle set by a Zen master

means I must become more agile and move more quickly, and be compact like a small man. But this goes without saying. No, he said "become" a small man. This is a very teasing riddle. Why can't he be straightforward with me? Why always this subtle innuendo?

Sitting alone in the center of the communal dining hall, picking at the rice and shredded vegetable meal, my mind became busy, and I began to realize that my entire body was aching. No doubt, from the hour-long free fighting. A couple of friends called me to join them at their table, but I rejected the invitation, saying that I needed to go to bed.

Try as I may, sleep wouldn't come. Although my body was tired, my mind was like an electric kaleidoscope that I could not turn off. Growing more and more restless, I finally gave up the idea of sleep, dressed, and walked out into the Tokyo night.

A sense of loneliness pervaded my entire being. "Here I am in the middle of a busy, colorful metropolis, but why do I feel so alone? What am I doing here?" I thought. "With Saturday Drawing closer, I feel further away from myself than I have ever felt." A large amusement center decked in alluring neon signs drew me in. In the far corner of the game-filled area was a group of boisterous individuals crowded around an electronic game called "Racing Car." These were the biggest Japanese men I had ever seen. I gravitated to the opposite corner of the establishment, trying to appear inconspicuous.

Hardly had I slipped the *yen* coin into the game of "Space Invaders" when I heard a booming voice. "Ah, karate man, you come here!"

I looked up, and sure enough, a beefy man was waving good-bye to me. I had recently learned that this gesture meant "come here." I considered running out and escaping but, on second thought, I walked across to them wondering how they knew about my karate. I didn't have to wait long for an answer.

"What *dojo* you attend?" asked the same man, pointing to the Japanese characters inscribed on my T-shirt. I told him, and they did not seem over-interested. Then a Japanese girl among them said to me, "You very tall man."

"Yes," butted in the full of a man, "but he very skinny."

They roared in delight. I forced a smile, bowed to them, and headed for the door. A westerner who had been watching turned to me, saying, "Don't feel bad; those are *sumo* wrestlers. It's just their way of being friendly."

"It served me right," I thought to myself. "I wanted to know what is small man. Now I know, or do I?"

I walked on and on thinking of all my friends back home, my dojo, my sensei, and if there was any time I needed them, it was now. The distance was so far. Distance is that gap separating two entities, but what is distancing?

Chapter 21

Third *Dan* Grading—A Fight to Close the Distance Between Self and Reality

Hundreds of shoes and straw sandals covered the floor and stairs of the *dojo*. The floor was a hive of activity. There were three groups, each with a huge crowd of *karateka* gathered around, watching and grading. Other *karateka* warmed up and practiced in any small free space they could find. I found Gary and Seto. Gary looked pale. "When do Gary and I go on?" I asked Seto.

"Much later," said Seto. "Still about 150 people going for *shodan* and then about 80 *nidan*."

It was now about 10:30 in the morning. Watching two university brown belts in *kumite* made me feel uneasy. They were good. "If the brown belts are this good, imagine what the third *dan* grading will be like," I remarked. Seto pulled us away, inviting us for a snack downstairs. "Still plenty of time," he pointed out.

In the afternoon, we watched those going for nidan. Tanaka, who was also dressed in karate *gi* was testing the *nidan* candidates, not by marking them on paper, but by fighting them. He must have participated in about 20 or 30 fights that afternoon, all of which he took in his stride. His opponents seemed desperate as he easily dispatched them with leg sweeps, throws, or stinging blows to their bodies. A few times, he literally slapped his opponent's cheeks with his roundhouse kicks, which came from nowhere.

Among the *nidans* was one very aggressive and spirited individual by the name of Kaneko. In both of his fights, he knocked out his opponents with a right-footed roundhouse to the jaw. I didn't like the look of him. He was dangerous and only went forwards. I made a mental note to be careful of that right foot.

The next few hours we walked up and down the stairs from *dojo* to restaurant. I couldn't stomach anything more than *miso-shiru.** It was five o'clock when the three groups formed into one area. At a long line of tables were seated the most senior karate men in the world. My nerves were raw by the time my name was called out.

There were five of us facing the *shihankai*—Gary, myself, Sado, and two other Japanese who were from outside the Tokyo area. Each of us was required to do our favorite *kata*.

Gary went on first. He did *Nijushiho*. Midway through, he lost balance slightly. Not a murmur came from the thousand eyes focused upon his every move. It was rather like the mobs that gather around famous golf players to watch a $100,000 putt. There was one difference today—this crowd was almost within touching distance of Gary. The grading area was very small.

Sado's *kata* was pure power, not pretty, but performed with total effort and focus.

My turn came. I stood in the middle of the small arena waiting for the command to begin. The examiners were discussing Sado's *kata*. My legs felt like rubber; they trembled, and there was nothing I could do about it. I felt the perspiration running down my cheeks. The master told me to begin. I announced my *kata*, "*Gankaku.*" My voice echoed loudly across the *dojo*. I bowed. The sound of my sweat droplets pounding the floor was magnified by the silence. There are times in *Gankaku* when one stands like a crane standing on a rock. This is where the *kata* derived its name. After a series of fast moves, one has to suddenly change into a smooth, flowing rhythm of graceful moves, whereby one leg is drawn up behind the knee of the other leg, and balancing on one leg for a time, one then slowly swivels around and delivers a snapping high side kick.

I finished the *kata*, and to this day cannot recall the details. How good it was I will never know.

It was similar with the *kumite*. There was no time for thinking. One of the Japanese in my group faced Kaneko, the aggressive

---

* *miso-shiru*—bean soup

nidan, who immediately felled him with the most potent round-house to the jaw I had ever seen. Again, that right foot. The grading of my colleague had started and ended within seconds, as he was in no condition to continue. So this is what Gary had meant. Kaneko, of course, had nothing to lose. His grading was already over. I rationalized that if my colleague could not cope with a second *dan*, he was then not yet ready to become a third *dan*. One thing had become clear. I now understood the rules of this game, and that was all I knew and needed to know, for in this moment my attitude suddenly changed. I went cold, but deadly cold.

My name was called, and what I had been fearing happened. Kaneko stepped out to face me. As we were told to start, he stepped in, and I instinctively moved backwards. I felt the roundhouse as it glanced off my right cheek—he had used his left foot. I didn't see it, but fortunately had managed to ride the blow by sliding backwards. I had retreated and fallen into the ring of people watching. Walking back to the center line, I told myself that I must only go forwards; otherwise, I had no chance.

On *hajime*, we both shot forwards simultaneously, but my leading punch must have been a fraction of a second quicker than his kick. He dropped to the ground like a dead bird and there he lay. A voice from the judges panel shouted, "More control!" I bowed and waited, not believing what had happened, for I had definitely not followed through with the technique. I must have touched a nerve center on his jaw. Kaneko stood up looking slightly dazed. I then faced the other Japanese from my group. We had a couple of clashes in which we both attacked and blocked each other. Finally, I surprised myself by back-kicking him into the crowd. It was a well controlled blow delivered just as he was losing balance. How I did it I still don't know. I happened to be in the right place at the right time. Is this what Tanaka meant by distancing? But still my inner voice persisted, "What is distancing?"

My other fights went reasonably well as I began to feel a sense of control over my emotions. "Maybe this too has something to do with distancing,"" I thought, "like getting closer to one's true self." I almost felt ready to meet Sado, but fate works in its own strange

way. All that training, those explosive confrontations, the worrying, the buildup, and now, instead, I faced Tabata *Sensei* for my
last fight. He had recently returned from overseas. For his opening
gambit, he feinted by circling his open hands in front of my face,
suddenly switching to a powerful leg sweep that sent me tripping
over my own feet in a sideward direction. But I recovered balance
before I fell, only to be caught a second time by the same tactic. "I
must wake up," I said to myself, as we were directed back to the
center of the area, for in the very moment I thought I understood
what distancing was, I was in that instant too distanced away from
myself to perceive what was happening. On hajime, I opened with
a front kick, which Tabata blocked powerfully. He tried to sweep
again with his massive right foot. I avoided it by sliding backwards
and suddenly out of nowhere came the favorite technique I had
been practicing so hard. My left leg started off as a front kick, and
my opponent started blocking downward as before, but suddenly
my foot changed from a forward direction to a round action. My
roundhouse kick neatly tapped him on the side of his jaw. I showed
no emotion, but felt ecstatic inside. "Another mistake," I reminded
myself. His eyebrows lifted, and his eyes went wide with surprise.
He chuckled heartily and slapped me on the back, saying, "Oh,
very good technique."

The examiner cut in, "*Hajime!*" Tabata switched on instantly,
swept me into a horizontal position, and before I landed, scored *ippon* with a powerful, controlled blow to the chest.

"*Yame!*" ordered the chief examiner.

I bowed to the gentle giant who stood in front of me smiling. I
respected him deeply for his skill but more so for his sincere
warmth and benevolent way. "He is truly a big man." I felt this
emotion strongly. "He has a soft side; he is humble. Is this not
what the master meant when he implied that I become the small
man? I have been too filled with myself. This is my hardness. That
is why I often miss the actions of others. I have got to learn to see
clearly. And isn't this type of seeing intimately related to distancing?"

Chapter 22

Loneliness and Discovering Something Truly Precious

The gradings ended, and no results were given. This was the way of Japanese karate. Results were seen as unimportant. As I walked across the empty dojo floor, I though of a Japanese proverb: "Live with cause, leave results to the great law of the universe." Although I knew there was much wisdom in these words, I was unable to shed myself of a deeply implanted habit. I was dying to know whether I had passed or failed. I had probably failed, I reasoned. But I badly needed to know on which side my coin lay.

On the stairs, I passed a group of instructors. Tabata *Sensei* reached out and pulled me to a halt. "You come for dinner."

"*Sensei*, I must go and pack. I leave tomorrow." A lame excuse, but I was now overcome with a state of anti-climax. I felt empty inside and didn't want to impose my blankness upon the *senseis*. What's more, it required effort to communicate with this group, and my understanding of Japanese was limited. Mostly, we talked in sign language, in very elementary English and, for my part, in very broken Japanese.

Seto and Oishi grabbed me and dragged me along while Tanaka warned, "Tonight no sleep...last time in Japan must enjoy...sleep on plane. Okay! We help you pack...not worry!"

Sitting next to Tabata in the taxi, I kept waiting for a suitable opening in the conversation to ask him the nagging question. But no such opening presented itself, and soon we joined the instructors at an "Eat-and-Drink-as-Much-as-You-Like-in-Two-Hours" type of restaurant. I was still not my total carefree self.

As we began with the singing of songs, Tabata sat next to me, and, raising his glass to me, said quietly, "I think maybe tomorrow you *sandan*." Before I could say anything, he joined in with the singing, indicating that I should sing louder. His ambiguous comment had not relieved my inner nagging.

From that moment, I resolved to convert my self-centeredness to an outward spirit. After all, it was my last night in Japan. I sang and even did a dance for the instructors, which apparently looked so ridiculous that we ended by literally rolling on the floor with laughter.

I don't remember how I got home, but I was awakened the next morning by Seto's telephone call. As we spoke, my eyes surveyed the room, and it gradually occurred to me that the nature of its contents had changed drastically.

"Please wash and dress. Be ready in 30 minutes."

"Where are you?" I asked in a dazed voice.

"Downstairs. I take you to the airport," said Seto.

As I replaced the receiver, I noticed that all my belongings had disappeared. That is, except for my red suitcase and black overnight bag, which stood side by side in the middle of the neatly tidied room.

At the airport, I shook Seto's hand and thanked him for everything. He produced the large carrier bag filled with parcels that were wrapped in gaily colored paper and complete with attractively tied bows.

"From all instructors," he said, and before I could answer, he handed me a large brown envelope, pushing me forwards into the area restricted to passengers.

"Please, you only open envelope when plane in sky," he added.

I was caught up in a wave of passengers moving forwards, clinging to the bags and parcels precariously dangling from all sides. As I was about to turn into the first passageway, I heard his voice, "*Sayonara*." Turning, I saw his face clearly for an instant, and then it was swallowed by the crowd.

"*Sayonara*," I said quietly to myself as I walked down the long corridor. "*Sayonara*, my dear friend."

Thoughts of tiredness were non-existent as the droning of the takeoff jets had lulled me into the deepest sleep. "We have just reached the halfway mark." The voice seemed to come from far off, but as I awoke I realized that the captain was speaking to us over the intercom.

On my lap lay the brown envelope Seto had given me. As I began opening it, I felt a touch on my shoulder.

"Do you know you have slept for over eight hours and missed two meals? Aren't you hungry?" asked the smiling air hostess.

My hands slowly unfolded the large, white rice paper *sandan* certificate. It was inscribed with bold, black Japanese characters.

"You seem far away." She leaned forwards speaking into my ear. "You still have a long way to go. Let me bring you something to eat."

"Really?" said I without thinking. "Yes, I do still have a long way to go, but at least I'm beginning to enjoy it all."

Part 2

An Analysis

1. Karate-do—A Play Form Which Has the Potential For Communicating Something Valuable to Man

In essence, the story in this book is concerned with communication. It represents the awakening of human awareness, of one individual reaching out to another, sharing an experience and in the process, finding himself. The story depicts living beings participating in life, engaged in what J. Huizinga believes, "Is one of the main bases of civilization"—play. True play is an activity that transcends the restrictive bounds of material existence even though it is always governed by rules, natural or man-made.

Generally, public life in its material form does not easily permit mistakes and weaknesses. The spirit of friendship is rarely present. The human who errs is generally punished by society's mechanistic, unforgiving spirit, which manifests itself in rigid labels, laws, and norms. It is not so much the physical side of the punishment to which I refer, but rather the manner in which the punishment is effected. Punishments range from imprisonment to being sniggered at by a group of people who are different from oneself.

It is chiefly this second kind of non-accepting attitude to which I refer.

1.1 Communication Which Fosters Understanding and Awareness

The story deals with the spirit of friendship, implied or explicit. There was awareness of freedom and choice. With regard to freedom and choice, K. Roelofse comments that "Man has the freedom to act like an angel, or like the devil himself." Furthermore, Roelofse points out that man can transcend the restrictive bounds of animal existence, thus enhancing the quality of human existence, giving it dignity.

There is, in addition to freedom and choice, an underlying sense of dignity present in the story. Kierkegaard believed that, "The highest degree of resignation that a human being can reach is to acknowledge the given independence in every man..." This statement is powerful, for this type of serenity is not passive. In terms of communication, it means reciprocal sharing of one another's horizons.

It is impossible for me to acknowledge the given independence in another unless I am first aware of the unique part of that person's being. If I become aware of what is different in another being, then I have, in that instant, learned something of value. I have then added to my horizon of understanding an extra awareness. This, then, is a form of re-creation for me for I have, of my free will, created a new truth. I needed to be aware and open in order to do this for myself. Any other form of learning is manipulation.

Whether or not I decide to use what I learned from an experience with another person will be dependent upon my personal freedom to choose what I will to do, and, in ideal form, whether I believe that acting on the new information will enhance and dignify my existence, or not. Thus, if I desire the freedom to choose and map out my destiny, I must allow the same for others—not be judgmental of their spirit and behavior, but rather be aware of it— offering them guidance should they desire it. Basically, to achieve this state, I need to cultivate a forgiving spirit which is, in essence, friendly and has an element of love present. Before I can begin to truly forgive others, I need to forgive myself. This is not easy to achieve. Therefore, I need wise teachers and friends to help me to interpret life. Of course, parents, family, friends, and teachers are our initial interpreters of life. But it is often at these early stages that, along with wisdom, we also learn foolishness, and this foolishness can be passed on to us unwittingly by someone close to us.

1.2 Communication Which Blocks Understanding and Awareness

Millman shows how a seemingly innocent remark, "Sammy, you're clumsy," repeated a number of times by a well-meaning mother, caused problems later for Sammy, who kept losing balance during gym exercise. When Millman encouraged him to master the movement, Sammy smiled sheepishly, saying, "I am sorry, but I am a clumsy person." In effect, Sammy's mother had not forgiven him for spilling milk or whatever—errors which even the greatest athletes make. Thus, Sammy was carrying a "ghost" or illusion around with him, which was a barrier to his natural awareness for learning.

I have had many so-called "clumsy," "stupid," "useless" Sammys in my karate classes who, fortunately, were able to transcend these illusory terms and become highly aware and skillful human beings with realistic self images. Sammy's problem stemmed from an emotional barrier clouding his awareness. This prevented him from enjoying the freedom of movement that a form of play such as gymnastics offers. What is important is that it was through this form of play that his awareness problem was both discovered and solved.

Sammy was retarded, in a sense, emotionally. Everybody is retarded in some way and to some degree. I refer now to the body (movement and health): mind (understanding and evaluation); and spirit or emotional state (life giving energy). The concepts of freedom, choice, and awareness are closely related to the three above areas of one's being. In other words, if there is a weakness in any area of the being, it will no doubt have some effect on the rest of the organism. A weakness is seen as something which restricts freedom to choose or act, or both. When one is robbed of movement, whether it be bodily, mental, or emotional movement (energy), one is robbed of life and well-being.

1.3 Play—An Ideal Mode of Humanistic Communication

Marshall McLuhan says that our technological extensions numb us. They tend to diminish normal movement of mind or body. For instance, if I allow a computer to do all my thinking for me, it will put my mind at rest, thus robbing me of my freedom to think. Unless I engage in some form of testing mental activity, it would be like putting my mind in a sling, and any part of the body which is immobilized atrophies over a time. A Chinese proverb supports the idea of movement and life: "The door pivot in a happy house will never be worm eaten."

Thus, I wish to postulate that in order to gain a sense of well-being, we need to constantly resculpt ourselves, and we should become artists in doing so. Unlike a statue or painting, the human being is an ongoing organism that needs constant care and attention. According to Huizinga, play is "...a necessity both for the individual...and for society." Children need play as much as they need food and water. Similarly, adults need play in order to re-create, re-shape, and re-energize their psyches and physiques. Some forms of play are more all-embracing than others. Throwing darts is a play form which may result in certain benefits, but it is a far cry from squash, which involves a greater involvement of the human organism. The general benefits, of course, speak for themselves. In other words, we need suitable environments for learning, re-creating, and re-energizing our nerves and our muscles. In terms of communication, we need to learn through whatever medium cultivates maximum awareness.

1.4 Experiencing Reality—A Fresh Self Awareness

Kierkegaard believed that true understanding came from actual participation. He gained this idea from the Bible, "Be ye doers of the word not hearers only." This is his existential message, that we need to exist in whatever we are learning.

Musashi, (known as the sword saint of Japan) was such a man. He is a legend and an inspirational figure in the Japanese martial arts. He was a wandering warrior who won all 31 of his duels to the death, yet he passed away naturally, leaving as heritage one valuable publication, the *Book of Five Rings*. He had a simple, yet effective philosophy. he never bypassed a master of any art or profession without learning from him, and in turn, teaching. He was a living example of the idea of being at once master and student. He believed that a warrior's path was strategy. I was told that he said, "There is no way to the truth—truth is the way." He believed that it was good to learn from history and traditions, but that in times of immediacy and interaction, one needed to transcend tradition and to forget all learning in order to allow one's own inner creative spirit to act. This type of action is spontaneous, free from good and evil, free from ego. It is more than re-creation; it is pure creation—quality action which flows freely from the Creator of all things. This is the quality of the freedom and awareness for which many of us are striving without even knowing it, yet it mostly eludes our grasp.

There is no guarantee that any form of art or play can take us beyond the realms of physical, mental, and emotional awareness into the higher states of spiritual awareness. Even enlightened spiritual leaders say that it is only God who, ultimately, can effect that change. However, while we exist in this physical universe we still have the choice to re-create or destroy ourselves, and to pursue activities which can help or hurt our well-being.

I believe that karate is an advanced play form which offers extremely great potential for self-development and awareness. I agree with Frank Foulkes that "karate is ideally suited to accomplishing this inner work." He believes it teaches unified action of mind and body, develops the spirit, deals in an individual manner with the relation between self and other and is intimately concerned with the problem of life and death.

2. Karate—A Play Form Which Communicates

The art of karate is at once a dynamic parallel activity to the game of life as well as being a representation of a higher set of ideals for human interaction and existence. A quote attributed to Gichin Funakoshi, founder of modern-day karate is, "The ultimate aim of the art of karate lies not in victory or defeat but in the perfection of the character of its participants."

Karate's energizing element is the involved interplay between human beings. It may thus be viewed as an existential form of communication which invites and requires individuals to become aware of themselves and others.

Two simple models will be used t examine the form of karate-do and its living content.

The first model aids us to become more aware of its potential as a communicable form. The second model will help us to understand the communicative play arena of karate—expressed through humanistic involvement—the involvement of student with teachers, colleagues, and nature.

2.1 The Communicative Potential of Karate

The chapters of this book may be considered to represent human growth from childhood to maturity. The contents represent the quest by beings to raise themselves above the drudgery of life to higher levels of well-being.

Karate parallels this ideal by its very structure and form.

Play is Represented as a Ladder

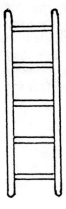

On its own, the ladder is a mere structure.

Two children appear and perceive the ladder. The situation has changed—we now have an object and two observers. The ladder provides potentialities for the children, not yet actualized.

One child climbs up a rung or two, enjoys this new awareness, then jumps off. The other child is inspired by this idea and does the same, only he climbs a little higher. Soon both of them are climbing, jumping, falling, praising themselves and each other, challenging and laughing. All the time they progress higher. In this interaction, potentialities become actualized.

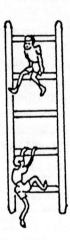

Taylor explains that, "through responsible decision, the self moves from a state of potentiality (non-being) to actuality (being)." The ladder (as a form) has provided healthy play. This is communication between beings in its most natural form—it is existential communication—with both sharing an experience, and at the same time competing and elevating awareness, skill, confidence, friendship, and respect for each other. They are heroes in a sense, to each other and to themselves. This type of participatory play is a civilized form of communication.

The bully or cheat who pushes over the ladder shatters civilization. He is not adhering to the rules (implied or other) of the game. He has intruded and manipulated them, robbing the players of the most important states of human awareness, namely, freedom to create and play, and he has in a real sense, robbed them of their dignity. Huizinga feels that "in the absence of the play spirit, civilization is impossible."

Karate-do may also be regarded as a ladder or a form, a ladder of potentialities and actualities. Like the children's ladder, it is both in structure and potential, essentially heroic.

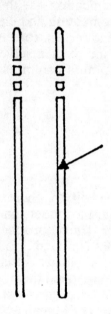

The uprights represent karate's cause, which is unlimited. This idea is indirectly communicated by the fact that there is no end to the *dan* ranks. This implies a reaching up to greater spiritual heights. This potential is represented by:
• The *dan* ranking system
• Championships
• Standards of excellence
• Status, etc.

The rungs represent results
(actualities):
• Rank achieved
• Championship wins
• Instructor status
• Other status awards and
  honors

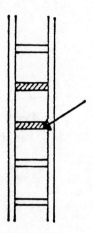

The spaces represent existential
arenas of action and interaction
(training, learning, interaction
with nature, tests, social interaction, championships, gradings,
etc.). The spaces represent the
dynamic areas of play involving
the individual in intersubjective
fashion. (This will be the expanded
area for examination in 2.2,
2.3, and 2.4.)

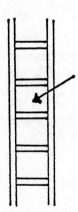

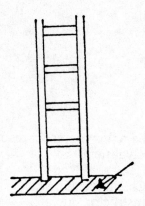

The ground or foundation on which the ladder is secured, is the world.

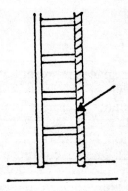

The substance from which the ladder of karate is formed is the spirit in which it was created. In other words, the actions of its creators, pioneers, and propagators.

The quality of this substance is a balanced blend of hard and soft—hard testing confrontations, balanced with warm healing relationships—true play. The finest swords grow out of a tempering fire and water. The substantialities of the ladder of *karate-do* is an ongoing factor, dependent upon the quality of interaction between *karate-ka* of each era

Unlike the ladder on which the two children played, the ladder of karate is not a fixed material form. If the quality of the ladder is always re-created by dedicated leaders and trainees, keeping in mind human freedom, dignity and excellence, then the play form karate will survive and grow, enduring the winds of change, thus providing a noble play arena for the re-creation and elevation of awareness and dignity in its participants. Huizinga said, "If our modern puerilism were genuine play, we ought to see civilization returning to the great archaic forms of recreation where ritual, style, and dignity are in perfect unison." This the heroic cause of *karate-do* as a whole, but a problem lies now in the smaller ladders which are being constructed all over the world. Many of these are the new *dojos* and organizations which spring up like mushrooms and all too often die just as fast. These are created by so-called instructors who, without going through sufficient tempering, erect shaky ladders on which their students play and too often hurt themselves physically and psychologically.

I conclude this view of karate-do by simply saying that karate is an all-embracing, highly beneficial play form provided that the instructor is truly qualified; that the organization to which he belongs has a reputable historical background; and finally that the instructor truly has his students' well-being at heart.

2.2 The Communicative Play Arena of Karate

This model is concerned with the awareness of the outer and inner man. The following extract illustrates how the human qualities of increased perception, creativity, and striving to maintain personal dignity can be brought to the fore through a highly intense play interaction:

I remember the words of my sensei, "They will seek kyo in you and attack kyo (weakness)."

Sado, I now realized, had managed to capture my spirit. During the warm-up, I spoke to myself, rationalizing that he was only flesh and blood like me and that I had only two alternatives: to stand up to him or be completely trodden under foot. Through all of the conditioning training, my mind was not totally present in my body...my mind had leapt ahead to the kumite training that I knew was inevitable...Sado became my invisible opposition...(from watching Sado) I decided that he was open to a left front kick. I planned to approach him timidly, (during the line work) suddenly create spirit by kiaiing (shouting) loudly, pause and a split second later deliver my front kick. (It worked (cf. Chapter 17).

This is an example of a human whose security and dignity is threatened, yet his creativity is stimulated, resulting in true action. His conflict with Sado was an awareness battle.

According to Kierkegaard, "Only the person who personally understands something cannot be misled, whereas any other person can be..." By misleading Sado, the writer had re-created within himself a sense of security and dignity and, in turn, communicated this truth to Sado.

We now step from the ladder into the action arena of karate play.

I. Represents the student's
   arena of life.
II. The student's arena of
   karate.

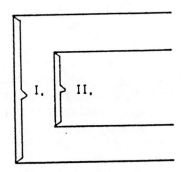

III. The student's inner creative
   world (spiritual).
IV. The observable physical
   self and environment of
   the student.

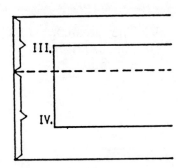

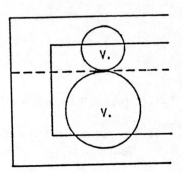

V. (The figure 8) represents the student's involvement in the karate arena, which impinges on life.

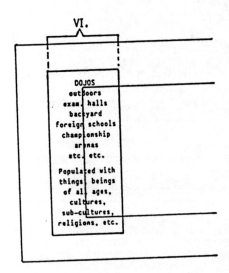

VI. The sub-arenas of play populated with beings and things.

VI.

DOJOS
outdoors
exam. halls
backyard
foreign schools
championship
arenas
etc. etc.

Populated with
things beings
of all ages,
cultures,
sub-cultures,
religions, etc.

2.3 Prime Categories of Play in Karate

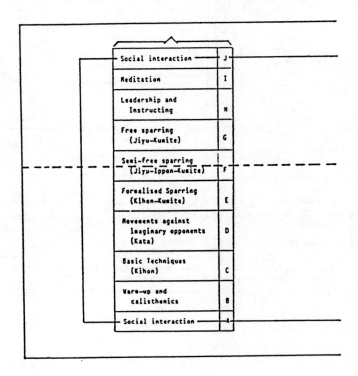

Social interaction	J
Meditation	I
Leadership and Instructing	H
Free sparring (Jiyu-Kumite)	G
Semi-free sparring (Jiyu-Ippon-Kumite)	F
Formalised Sparring (Kihon-Kumite)	E
Movements against imaginary opponents (Kata)	D
Basic Techniques (Kihon)	C
Warm-up and calisthenics	B
Social interaction	A

2.3 ⌐ PRIME CATEGORIES OF PLAY ⌐ **2.4** FORMS OF PLAY

Prime Category	Code		Forms of Play		
Social Interaction	J	FREEDOM	Communication in terms of well-being		
Meditation	I		Communication in terms of being alone		
Leadership and Instructing	H		An expression by self within bounds of the situation		
Free Sparring	G		Creative interplay between two fighters in varying situations.	Dojo fighting, Championships, Gradings, etc.	
Semi-Free Sparring	F		A greater variety of variables are introduced into competitive situations between protagonists.	Participants are free to use own strategies within limits.	
Formalised Sparring	E		A variety of games set by the instructor.	These are games in which techniques are used in competitive spirit against opponents.	
Movements against imaginary opponents	D	CONTROL	A game of visualizing possibilities.	Much like creative role-playing in which children engage.	Competitions in Kata against others.
Basic Techniques	C		Learning and performing the basics: play emerges as participants strive to kick higher, move faster, look better, keep going longer ..... target work to achieve accuracy, etc.		
Warm-up and Calisthenics	B		Strengthening Strength – Stamina – Agility, etc.	Done through co-operative play OR competitive play (or a subtle blend of both)	
Social Interaction	A		Communication in terms of circumstances.		

2.4 Forms of Play in Karate

This is a breakdown of the various types of play which take place within each of the categories of play. Listed above are only a few of the numerous possibilities, some of which were revealed in part one.

We will now study examples of each of the above categories and forms of interplay.

A. Social Interaction — Communication in Terms of Circumstance

The various karate arenas draw different types of individuals into intersubjective relationships. The *gasshuku* is one such example:

While eating breakfast, I realized how tightly knit our group had grown. Lisa and the girls washed the utensils and set the table while Lucas and Jack scouted for wood...Nick chose to be the chef.

Mannie pointed out that Nick, although an excellent cook, happened to be a messy one. He thus took it upon himself to keep our camp in a clean and livable condition...(cf. Chapter 4).

B. Warm-up and Calisthenics

An example of natural awareness of the other and self through play:

Lying on my back, opening and closing my legs, I became aware of the mixed group with whom I found myself. Next to me was a young, dark girl smoothly and lithely doing her exercises, while on the other side of her was a thick-set man, probably in his forties, puffing and blowing with much effort. To the front was a small boy who was so taken in by the sub-instructor's movements that he kept throwing himself off balance in his enthusiasm to emu-

late him. As I changed to the press-up position, drops of sweat splashed on the floor. I became more fascinated by the design the droplets formed on the floor than by the realization that my fellow students were all so different (cf. Chapter 1).

C. *Kihon*—Basic Techniques

Notice that at every stage of karate, *kihon* is always present. All that differs is the arena of practice. Each arena demands a different kind of awareness intimately involving one in a game against self and others. A good example of a change in awareness through a different *kihon* arena was the time the writer was invited to train in the black belt club. This is an example of play that takes place on a higher tight rope and virtually demands increased awareness in the participants. "As we started the *kihon* training, I immediately felt the difference in pace. I was behind the others..." (cf. Chapter 7).

D. *Kata*—Movements Against Imaginary Opponents

A form of role playing.

Kata is meant to exercise one's powers of imagination and visualization. Both the competitive and cooperative spirit of play are harmoniously present in this next excerpt, which[is an example of a creative intersubjective relationship between two beings. The brown belt grading arena brought this to the fore when Neville and the writer were being examined for excellence. "For a moment, during the midpoint of the *kata*, it occurred to me that this virtual stranger and I were working in unison. It was if we were Siamese twins, connected by an inner pulse from which I could not separate myself." (cf. Chapter 6)

E. *Kihon-kumite*—Formalized Sparring

A good example of play and awareness in the different arenas of *kihon-kumite* (formalized sparring) is in Chapter 2, when the *sensei* created a series of different approaches (slight changes to the game and rules) during the five-step sparring which took place between Stephen and the writer. The different approaches were that the students were encouraged to become more aware of themselves in demonstrating the concepts of air, water, fire, and earth. This is an existential playing with concepts—like the imaginative role playing which children and adult performers engage in. Park states, "Everyone is always, more or less, consciously playing a role...it is in these roles that we know ourselves. In a sense...this mask represents the conception we have formed of ourselves...the role we are striving to live up to...this mask is our truer self..."

Stephen suddenly transformed from a body of lightness into coiled spring steel. As my blocking forearm met his extending arm, I became aware of his inherent strength, because my arm bounced ineffectually off his, causing me to stumble and lose balance.

(Then to the water approach.) Facing each other again, Stephen's countenance changed. He had a relaxed look about him which caused me to relax...and that proved to e a mistake... (cf. Chapter 2).

The above play is aimed at making the participant aware of various states of tension and relaxation which he is later free to use in any situation—be it in or out of the *dojo*.

F. Jiyu Ippon Kumite—Semi-free Sparring

This is a category of play which demands increased awareness and creativity. The following incident took place in the *dojo*, but he way in which the play was conducted put pressure on the writer. This illustrates the idea of arenas created by human spirit (in this case created by the *sensei* and the other instructors):

My forearm was swollen from blocking... I had been winded by John once and decided that a sore forearm was a better proposition than rolling around on the floor, struggling to get air into a par of deflated lungs.

The thunderclouds building up within me reached their darkest one night, when I felt as if every member of the class was out to eat me alive, including my friend, Lucas. I...was not faring well. Suddenly I was hit on the nose, just hard enough to bring a few tears to my eyes. Something snapped within me; a spiritual metamorphosis took place...I moved forward against the current, looking through my opponents without seeing them...doing what I needed to do...and then, the one ray of sunlight within the storm: "Good, very good!" spoken by the sensei. *"You have made a breakthrough." (cf. Chapter 9)*

The above illustrates the semi-free and free stages where the *sensei* begins to impart truth and awareness in an indirect method. In this case, he did not tell the writer how to deal with the problem. Instead, he created situations such as the one above, which caused the writer to exercise his inherent creative skills. In this situation, the instructor acted as "midwife," allowing the writer to give birth to his own truth, thus producing a new awareness, in effect a type of spiritual awareness—a clarity created by the participant engaging in an active communication situation.

G. *Jiyu Kumite* —Free Fighting

We now move into a delicate arena of human interaction, an area relying upon the integrity and judgment of the participant. This is the reason free sparring is normally engaged in from the *dan* levels upwards, in order to minimize the occurrence of injury.

The free fighting situations dealt with in this work are examples of the "what" and "how" of our actions. Kierkegaard comments, "the 'what;' it is the same thing which was said before perhaps many times previously, and so the old saying is true: there is nothing new under the sun, this old saying which nevertheless always remains new. But 'how' it is said—this is what is new."

Conversational *kumite* (the various "hows" of free fighting:

The first type I like to term free sparring. This relationship has the character of two people engaged in relaxed, sincere, open conversation...each interested in what the other has to say...with neither one trying to outdo the other.

The second kumite *I see as free fighting. The confrontation is antagonistic...an opposition of wills...true argument. In this type of relationship (game) the aim is to defeat the opponent through superior technique and strategy (cf. Chapter 4).*

The championship arena produces this second type of interplay:

Neville had set a bouncing rhythm, and I unconsciously followed suit. In other words, he was calling the tune, and I was dancing to it. All seemed to be going well when suddenly, after trying to do an acrobatic leap, I half slipped and like a missile, Neville flew at me as I was trying to regain balance, and his airborne left foot found my midriff. The crowd yelled. He had scored...
(The fight resumed.)
Suddenly he leapt at me. My left fist exploded, and like a dead weight, Neville dropped to the floor. A sense of panic gripped my chest (cf. Chapter 11).

When students fight against students, as above, the interplay can sometimes become wild and uncontrolled, like insults, especially when emotions are affected for any reason whatever, such as the crowd urging one to win.

The above type of interplay is like a chess game with one major difference, namely, degree of involvement and risk. According to Palmer, "in true experience (involvement)...(there is) the playful probing of the subject from different angles...(there) lies the willingness to risk everything and to be instructed by the subject matter itself." In chess, the involvement and risk are limited mostly to the participants' minds. The karate championship arena demands an involvement of the whole being.

Another kind of *kumite* is when the student spars with a master, like a type of lecture or Socratic discourse:

The fight opened with me, relaxed, moving to and fro. Tanaka had created a rhythm. He would move towards me and then a little away. He kept doing this. I watched him intently. The third time, he came close and dropped his guard...I threw a reverse punch at his open chest. He deftly swiveled to the side. I missed him and began standing up-. Catching my arm with one of his hands, he leapt into the air, entwining his legs around my unsteady hips and with sudden explosive force, he wrenched me downwards, flattening my back against the floor...Still trapped like a fly in a spider's web, I felt the sharp slap of a well controlled heel to my chest...At last, I began having sleepless nights (cf. Chapter 19).

When a master spars with a student, he will, when he feels the student is ready, begin to put extra pressure on the student—always more than the student thinks he himself can handle. A controlled blow is not always a blow which is pulled short of contact. Control is a relative word. If the student (whom Tanaka was sparring with) had been a child, he would have handled him gently. In the case of the writer, he tapped him hard enough to worry him. The blow is, in this case, seen as a blow of enlightenment causing the student to reflect and become more aware.

If there was ever any time in my life when my head could have been taken off my shoulders, it was then. Yet Oishi had acted with benevolence, a true sportsman. But what of Sado and some of the other unknowns? Could I rely on them? No, I couldn't afford to take that chance. A fear gripped me, and at that moment I resorted to prayer. Inwardly I asked, "God, help me. Please help me face up to these men. What must I do? Give me what I need." (cf. Chapter 17)

According to Heidegger, "questioning...is the way a man contends with and draws being into showing itself." Heidegger believes there are certain times when "we should do nothing, but rather wait..."

In the case of the above free fighting dilemma, the answer came sooner than the writer expected, and in physical form:

Strangely, at that point, the master called a halt and spoke to me.
"You...too much thinking...you look only with two eyes...don't forget your whole body is an eye." I did not quite understand, but his few words had given me spirit." (cf. Chapter 17)

The above illustrates what Taylor, on Kierkegaard, says about drawing one's awareness away from the living situation: "He (man) keeps existence away by thinking." And the writer captured the "mindless" natural state (which characterizes true awareness) for a moment during his third dan grading when: *I avoided it by sliding backwards and suddenly, out of nowhere, came the favorite technique I had been practicing so hard."* (cf. Chapter 21)

H. Leadership and Teaching

There is another arena or type of interplay inviting creativity and self-awareness of both self and other.

Whatever weaknesses I had began to manifest themselves in my students. At one time, I kept telling the class to bend their back knee over their big toe. I would demonstrate the technique, but still the class didn't improve. Then it struck me. With childish inno-cence, the youngest boy said, "But sempai, *you don't have your back knee over your big toe!"* (cf. Chapter 10)

In the above case, the teacher learns from his students. This is where student becomes teacher. Palmer, in discussing the concept of understanding, illustrates how Socrates, "instead of trying to weaken his opponent's arguments, he tries to find their true strength, so that his own understanding may be transformed." Fur-thermore, saying what you know out loud is a way of talking to yourself, sometimes with unexpected results.

This is an important concept in the arena of human communications, for even where there is a great deal of control within a play situation, there is still the chance for the implicit leader to indirectly or directly (as above) express creativity. For example, in the strictly controlled *kihon* class, *"the purple belt who had been striking the* makiwara, *was the driving force of the class" (cf. Chapter 1).* Thus, although he was not actually conducting the class, the purple belt was playing a role of an implicit leader by the dynamic way in which he applied his techniques.

I. Meditation

Communication in terms of being alone.

The term meditation has in a number of cases caused those who have little knowledge of karate to become judgmental, thus defining it by means of an erroneous label. A label is a singular idea used to describe a total thing or being. A typical label is, "He is bad."

Other examples of comments based on unfounded logic are: "In karate, they meditate; therefore, they are praying to some foreign god." "In karate, they bow; therefore, it is religion." "Karate comes from the East; therefore, it is evil."

Labels tend to point in one of two directions—what is judged good and acceptable, or what is judged evil and unacceptable.

I wish to demonstrate how the awareness of truth is destroyed through a judgmental form of reasoning which, in more realistic terms, is "unreasoning." Is it possible for any human being to be totally aware? I think not. What is significant is that some being are just that much more aware than others, and this is what survival is all about—degree of awareness. It is not religion, bows, rituals, meditation, or whatever fixed form of communication one may use, whether in business, play, working, karate, or any life activity.

In other words, meditation is just a word. It is neither good nor evil. It is merely a way of exercising awareness. Meditation is not religious, but it can be used in religion. Meditation is not necessarily good, but it can be used to elevate man. Meditation is not necessarily evil, but it can be used to destroy man.

Meditation is to reflect upon, to study, to ponder, to observe with intentness, to think, to exercise the mind.

All of the above describe awareness in some or other form, and this is the aim of meditation that karate encourages its students to engage in. It is not manipulating the student nor persuading him to think in any particular direction. It is, in fact, the total opposite, for it suggests that the student explores his very own inner world to re-discover himself, to be at peace within by being at peace with both others and nature. And, if he wishes, to communicate with God—his God, not some unreal karate god, which does not exist.

The above type of meditation is communication free of any manipulation. It allows the karate meditator freedom to pursue his own personal will. He is free to think about the practice, to work out a new move, to look at a tree or bird, to pray if he wishes, or to engage in no-thinking.

"No-thinking! This is evil," say certain judges of life, "for if you have a vacuum in your mind, then evil forces can take you over."

Well, they are right in a sense, for a vacuum connotes death. It is no-awareness. This is why judgments are all too often erroneous, for if we are now open enough to examine what no-thinking means, we will see clearly that it is one of the most important awareness states. Where Kierkegaard implied that thinking stops action, I agree and add that judgmental thinking stops immediate awareness. By judgmental, I mean the type of thinking which is destructive to man's well-being. It was the kind of thinking which God forbade Adam to engage in: "...you must not eat from the tree of the knowledge of good and evil."

My entire thesis, that the linking of eastern and western truths (which sometimes appear to be in conflict, but often convey similar messages), hinges upon these words. In terms of human awareness, both the above words of wisdom, and the pragmatic way of karate, lead to the common interest—human awareness. Both are saying, just be aware; do not judge. In other words, no-thinking does not mean vacuum (for this is death-state in terms of intra-communication). Funakoshi wrote, "As a mirror's polished surface reflects whatever stands before it and a quiet valley carries even small sounds, so must the student of karate render his mind empty of selfishness and wickedness in an effort to reach appropriately towards anything he might encounter."

This implies a no-thinking condition which is a state of being which perceives everything for what it is.

Some examples of no-thinking in meditation are, *"He (the sensei) would spend one week alone on his own gasshuku, 'emptying his cup,' as he put it. His existence involved doing what he felt attracted to doing and that, I am told, included not-doing." (cf. Chapter 4)*

This appears to be a contradiction, but it is an indirect way of communicating the idea of relaxed freedom. The west has tended to divide understanding into two extremes: good/evil; true/false; black/white; one/zero; which is ideal for scientific experimentation, but which certainly does not deal with states of awareness involving inner human truths.

I once asked a Japanese friend whether he thought advanced technology was a good or bad thing. He smiled, and merely answered, *"Mu."* It was explained to me that the question is incapable of being answered in any fixed way. Furthermore, it implies that it is neither good nor bad.

This answer is concomitant with the idea of not attaching a good/evil label to any thing or idea. *'Mu'* (no-thing) comes closest to the truth, for instead of being aware, like a label, it frees itself from definition by allowing the speaker or hearer to realize that there are things in the universe that no mind or computer can capture or evaluate—things like the magic of the moment.

The concept, "think," in terms of this discussion, is thus applying one's mind to things that have passed or defining some possibility for the future.

No-thinking is the ideal state for being aware of the present. A good driver does not focus his attention on hand and foot actions. He learned these previously. He is aware of his environment—

roads, vehicles, and people. In essence, his best actions stem from a no-thinking state. The driver who talks to others or is thinking about a problem (like the student who was involved in the driving incident and confrontation with another driver (cf. Chapter 11), is not only aware of the driving situation. The body of the great pianist knows technique; the mind knows music.

One of the arenas of meditation which is often empty of human awareness is nature—our Creator's art— the most worthy of all areas of involvement.

(After the hard climb up the mountain) My legs and lungs were burning from the climb. "A perfect spot for meditation," the sensei observed as he directed us to sit and quietly take in the scene. My strength and energy rapidly returned as I sat peacefully amidst this harmonious setting. The reality of nature with its paradoxical character of contrasts captivated me. The sharp jutting rocks were softened by the green ferns and oozing water (cf. Chapter 4).

J. Social Interaction—Communication in Terms of Well-Being

Like meditation, social interaction is one of the creative and restoring sources of energy for the individual. Where the training arenas may be viewed as the fire, so the meditative and social arenas are the water which help temper the participant, and in all probability, cause him to develop into a resilient and balanced person, aware of both his own qualities and weaknesses. Realizing one's human potential and gaining an understanding of life are closely dependent upon one's relationship with others.

A social interaction can occur on the *dojo* floor: *"Once, Oishi and I both slipped and fell in the sweat. I thought he would kill me, but he lay on the floor laughing, finally saying, 'You very clever fighter...make deep river...me nearly drown.' I found this very funny." (cf. Chapter 19)* The above interaction illustrates the forgiving spirit present in true play. This fosters well-being.

The following social interaction took place off the *dojo* floor:

"You come for dinner." "Sensei, I must go and pack. I leave tomorrow." A lame excuse...I felt empty inside and I didn't want to impose my blankness upon the senseis. What's more, it required effort to communicate with this group and my understanding of Japanese was limited.

Seto and Oishi grabbed me and dragged me along while Tanaka warned, "Tonight, no sleep...last time in Japan must enjoy...sleep on plane. Okay! We help you pack...not worry."

From that moment, I resolved to convert my self-centeredness to an outward spirit. I sang and even did a dance for the instructors, which apparently looked so ridiculous that we ended by literally rolling on the floor with laughter. (cf. Chapter 22)

What the above passage communicates is that humans need to enter many varied arenas in order to become more aware, and thus have a balanced view. How sad it would have been if the writer had given in to his self-centered state of depression and refused the kind invitation by the Japanese instructors to join their party. He would have missed the true purpose of all karate play—rounded character. He would have failed to see the softer human side of those "fighting machines." He would not have existed in their camaraderie. He would, no doubt, have cast a judgment on them as being exclusively cold, dangerous fighters.

Instead, he made friends. By accepting him, they bestowed upon him the most precious gift—not karate technique, but freedom. They helped him to counter-balance his newly found inner state of realization (of loneliness) developed through his recent karate encounters. They did this by reaching out to him in friendship and inviting him to respond. His joyful response was in itself a new awareness, a true expression of freedom.

2.5 The Teacher's Involvement With the Student

How the recipient becomes communicator:

Social interaction	J	
Meditation	I	
Leadership	H	**2.5.2 INDIRECT COMMUNICATIONS**
Free sparring	G	
Semi-free sparring	F	
Formalised sparring	E	
Forms (*kata*)	D	
Basics	C	**2.5.1 DIRECT COMMUNICATIONS**
Warm-up & Calisthenics	B	
Social interaction	A	

2.5.1 Direct Communication—Learning Forms

Play-types B, C, C, and E are to do with the learning and development of technical skills in the student. Therefore, they demand a more direct and explicit approach by the teacher (communication). For example, the teacher, handling the beginners' class, communicated in the following fashion: *"Relax your arm as you begin the blow and allow your outbreath to coordinate with the extending action of the arm. Now tense the hips and stomach and finish the outbreath as the fist reaches the end target point." (cf. Chapter 1)*

It is interesting to glance at the variety of forms on which *karate-do* is structured. The fact that these forms exist is, in itself, an indirect form of communication to the student, implying that it is for him to create for himself the content. Thus, the form is an outward representation of an inner truth. But, according to Condon, "meanings are in people," thus, they are not transmittable through direct communication.

A number of these forms are:

rei (the bow)	• a physical action which represents etiquette, respect for others and, finally, love.
yoi (be ready)	• represents the core idea of this thesis—awareness.
kiai (a shout)	• an outward representation of inner fighting spirit.
mokuso (meditation)	• a quiet, reflective time of awareness.

Note that the above forms are not only in word form (representations), but they go one step further and are deliberate actions (performances or presentations). One might say that ideas are being put into action, but how much inner meaning they convey to the performer will depend upon his degree of awareness of life, and what meaning he has personally attached to them. The parrot or ape could imitate the above forms, but his inner world may or may not be in a state of poverty. Therefore, these forms communicate both a direct truth as well as an indirect truth. They are pointers to how the human being may be elevated and thus freed from the shackles binding and threatening his survival.

2.5.2 Indirect Communication—Creative Involvement of the Student

Play-types F, G, H, I (and A and J) are more to do with fostering self-awareness and creativity within the student. This demands a more indirect communicational approach by the teacher. In effect, the teacher steps aside, reduces himself, and invites the student to make his own decisions. This is an invitation to self-creativity. The teacher changes from the dominant role of disciplinarian to the empathetic role of midwife. He helps create the ideal situation in order that the student may give birth to his own truth, so to speak. The true and unique artist emerges when creative excellence begins to flow freely from the real inner self.

There are many examples of indirect communication in this work. One of these was during a situation when the writer was training in the Japanese instructors' class and held a lazy, high stance.

The master approached a kenchusei *training next to me. I heard him shouting at the man. He happened to be in a very low stance. "More down...more lower!" The* kenchusei *replied with "Osu!" and looked as if he would disappear through the floor if he went any lower. The master kept doing this, and then it dawned on me that he was using English, speaking to a Japanese! He had never done this before. The penny dropped...so I dropped into a low stance. Immediately, the master left the tired* kenchusei *and moved away...(cf. Chapter 19)*

2.5.3 Teacher's Distancing and Timing

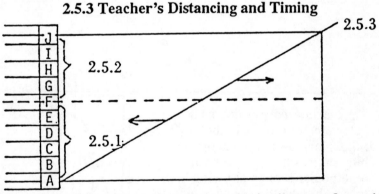

The diagonal line represents the teacher's distance from the student.

At certain times, the teacher is close (direct and physical communication); at other times, the teacher is distant in physical communication, yet close in spirit (indirect communication). These contrasts, in terms of communication, can occur within one training session as well as over a long period of time. The excellent teacher thus prods and draws the student into reaching elevated states of excellence and awareness.

2.5.4 The True Master Sacrifices Self

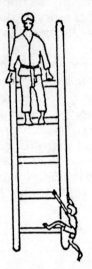

The teacher already stands on the ladder of *karate-do*. The beginner (seen as a child) approaches and is motivated to reach up and play upon the ladder (of karate possibilities).

The teacher reaches down and helps the child up onto the first rung. He shows him, encourages him, praises him, and reveals to him the dangers by allowing him to stumble; he then secures him and redirects him. The communicative approach primarily is direct.

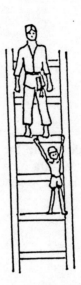

The child has grown stronger and more aware. He is higher on the ladder, playing more demanding and risky games. The teacher, who has himself progressed higher up the ladder, encourages the boy via help and personal example.

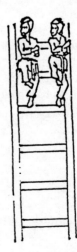

In time, the child matures into a dynamic adult. Now teacher and student progress up the ladder side by side—each sharing with the other some part of his own mastery.

With the passage of time, a stage
is reached where the teacher is
aware of a rung (goal) which he is
finally unable to reach on his
own.

The teacher invites the student
to climb on his back, giving the
student the awareness and
strength to reach greater
heights.

Thus, the excellent communicator accomplishes his work. These are the true masters of whom we all need to become aware in order to set free the hidden potentials that are within us.

There are so-called teachers (in any sphere of existence) who kick the student off the ladder— for whatever reason.

Then there are others who stagnate on one rung of the ladder and thus block the way up for the aspiring student. These are the spoilsports of the karate ladder of play and life. For, in spoiling play, they shatter civilization, they stifle human potential, freedom, and dignity and in the process block out awareness.

Conclusion

I am fortunate to be closely involved with so many genuine masters in some way or another. Without them, this book would not exist.

There is much that has been left unsaid. The state of human awareness is still pregnant with unimagined possibilities, and I ask forgiveness for any error which I may have unwittingly made. I have tried to demonstrate, through the resources of my own experience and study, a view of awareness that communicators in every field of endeavor should at least take a glance at, if not criticize and expand upon.

Kierkegaard said that a communicator should live in his communication, and that the communication of an inner truth should be posed as a contradiction—a dialectical knot—which the recipient is compelled to unravel, thus changing him into a communicator.

I exist both as a teacher and a student of karate. Both the student and the teacher in this story are me, and they are you. I know that I am at once master and fool—particularly the latter. But more than that, I am also the experiences and ideas of my students and masters with whom I have been closely involved.

This is the spirit of this book—friendship. It is not an autobiography. It is a fleeting glimpse at one side of awareness. There is also, of course, another side which is unstated, and which powerfully communicates of its own volition:

"Yes, I do still have a long way to go, but at least I'm beginning to enjoy it all.

Bibliography

Foulkes, F.R., (s.a.) *Karate—An Advanced Treatise.* (Still to be published). New York: Weatherhill Publishing Co.

Goffman, E. 1959. *The Presentation of Self in Everyday Life.* Middlesex: Penguin Books.

Huizinga, J. 1955. *Homo Ludens—A Study of the Play Elements in Culture.* Boston: The Beacon Press.

Kierkegaard, S. 1968. *Concluding Unscientific Postscript.* (Tr. by D.F. Swenson). Princeton: Princeton UP.

McLuhan, M. 1964. *Understanding Media.* London: Routledge & Kegan Paul Ltd.

Millman, D. 1979. *Whole Body Fitness—Training Mind, Body and Spirit.* New York: Clarkson N. Potter Inc.

Musashi, M. 1974. *A Book of Five Rings.* (Tr. by Victor Harris). New York: The Overlook Press.

Nakayama, M. 1967. *Dynamic Karate.* London: Ward Lock & Co., Ltd.

Nicol, C.W. 1975. *Moving Zen: Karate As a Way to Gentleness.* New York: William Morrow and Company.

Nishiyama, H. and Brown, R.C. 1960. *Karate: The Art of Empty-hand Fighting.* Tokyo: Charles E. Tuttle Co., Inc.

Nitobe, I. 1969. *Bushido: The Soul of Japan.* (Originally published in 1905). Tokyo: Charles E. Tuttle Co., Inc.

Palmer, R.E. 1969. *Hermeneutics—Interpretation Theory in Scheiermacher, Dilthey, Heidegger and Gadamer.* Evanston: Northwestern University Press.

Random, M. 1978. *The Martial Arts.* London: Octopus Books Ltd.

Reps, P. 1957. *Zen Flesh, Zen Bones.* Tokyo: Charles E. Tuttle Co., Inc.

Roelofse, K. 1981. "Human Communication—The Eloquence of Existence," *Communication*, Vol. 7, No. 1. Pretoria: University of South Africa.

Schmidt, S.O. 1976. *Karate—An Insight Into the Basic Concepts.* Johannesburg: Perskor Publishers.

Shoji, H. 1975. *Karate Kata Series—Gojushiho Sho.* Tokyo: TAK Inc.

Taylor, M.C. 1975. *Kierkegaard's Pseudonymous Authorship.* New Jersey: Princeton UP.

Van Schoor, M. 1980. *Kierkegaard and Communication.* Pretoria: H & R Academica (Pty) Ltd.

Watts, A. 1960. *The Spirit of Zen—A Way of Life, Work and Art in the Far East.* New York: Grove Press, Inc.

The Holy Bible. King James Version. Indianapolis: B.B. Kirkbride Bible Company Inc.

The Holy Bible. New International Version. New York: New York International Bible Society.